I0428080

BUDGET The United States
Department of the Interior

JUSTIFICATIONS

and Performance Information
Fiscal Year 2015

NATURAL RESOURCE DAMAGE ASSESSMENT AND RESTORATION PROGRAM

DEPARTMENT OF THE INTERIOR

Restoration Program
Assessment & Restoration Program

Fiscal Year 2015 Budget Justifications

TABLE OF CONTENTS

Appropriation: Natural Resource Damage Assessment and Restoration

Summary of Request   **Page**

Program Activities

NATURAL RESOURCE DAMAGE ASSESSMENT AND RESTORATION PROGRAM

GENERAL STATEMENT

FY 2015 Budget Request:

The Restoration Program's Fiscal Year 2015 request for current appropriations is $7,767,000, an increase of $1,504,000 over the 2014 enacted level of $6,263,000. The request supports modest increases in restoration support to increase on-the-ground restoration, and to increase the utilization of the growing balance of funds recovered in settlements to implement approved restoration plans. The 2015 request will also provide funding for training and to develop contingency plans that are required to respond to inland oil spills. These activities will be accomplished consistent with the recommendations of a detailed programmatic analysis and the development of a strategic plan currently underway, aimed at streamlining Restoration Program activities to maximize restoration outcomes. This analysis will seek to identify staffing constraints and process bottlenecks in the course of achieving restoration in coordination with our co-trustee partners. With the requested increase, staff will be added to the Program's Restoration Support Unit and allocated to bureaus and offices to accelerate restoration activities in accord with this expanding workload.

Over the last four years, the DOI Restoration Fund has received an average of over $135 million each year in restoration settlements and advanced or reimbursed cooperative damage assessment funds. The vast majority of these restoration settlements are shared jointly with other Federal, State, and tribal co-trustees, and as such, the Department cannot use them unilaterally. A number of long-running damage assessments cases have recently settled, and numerous others are currently in settlement negotiations. This sustained heightened influx of settlement funds is expected to continue as additional cases settle, and thus requires that the Restoration Program (along with involved DOI bureaus) examine its program infrastructure and staffing on a Department-wide basis, to best position the Program to deal with a growing pool of restoration settlement funds. The need for Program restructuring and additional staff resources will likely be further exacerbated by anticipated additional funds for ecological restoration from Restore Act activities and from a settlement for natural resource injury in the Deepwater Horizon oil spill once that damage claim is resolved.

The potential benefits associated with this budget request are significant, for both injured natural resources and for the American public's use and enjoyment of these resources. With nearly a half billion dollars in settlement funds currently residing in the DOI Restoration Fund, and more settlements on the horizon, moving forward deliberately and strategically in the implementation of restoration actions at dozens of sites nationwide will produce benefits, both ecologically and economically.

Total 2015 Budget Request
(Dollars in Thousands)

Budget Authority	2013 Actual	2014 Enacted	2015 Budget Request
Current	6,240	6,263	7,767
Permanent	68,502	79,424	80,000
TOTAL	**74,742**	**85,687**	**87,767**
FTE	*9*	*10*	*14*

Fiscal Year 2015 fixed costs of $39,000 are fully funded at the request level.

In addition, the request includes an estimate of $80.0 million in permanent funds for DOI bureaus and its Federal, State, and tribal co-trustees, which result from negotiated legal settlement agreements and cooperative damage assessments with responsible parties.

Executive Summary

The mission of the Natural Resource Damage Assessment and Restoration Program (Restoration Program) is to restore natural resources injured as a result of oil spills or hazardous substance releases into the environment. In partnership with other affected State, Tribal, and Federal trustee agencies, damage assessments provide the basis for determining the restoration needs to address damages to resources under public trust. Cooperation with its co-trustees and partners, and where possible, with the responsible parties, is an important component of meeting the Restoration Program's core mission.

As authorized by the Comprehensive Environmental Response, Compensation and Liability Act (CERCLA or Superfund), the Clean Water Act (CWA), and the Oil Pollution Act of 1990 (OPA), injuries to natural resources that the Department of the Interior manages or controls are assessed, and appropriate restoration projects are identified and carried out as part of negotiated settlements or in rare cases, litigation with potentially responsible parties. Recoveries, in cash or in-kind services, from the potentially responsible parties are then used to finance or implement the restoration of the injured resources, pursuant to a publicly reviewed restoration plan.

The Office of Restoration and Damage Assessment (Program Office) manages the confluence of the technical, ecological, biological, legal, and economic disciplines and coordinates the efforts of six bureaus and three offices to accomplish this mission. The Program has a nationwide presence encompassing nearly the full span of natural and cultural resources for which the

Secretary of the Interior has trust responsibility. Each bureau has unique natural resource trusteeship and brings its expertise to bear on relevant sites. The Restoration Program is a truly integrated Departmental program, drawing upon the interdisciplinary strengths of its various bureaus and offices, while eliminating or minimizing redundant bureau-level bureaucratic and administrative operations.

The **Bureau of Indian Affairs** is responsible for the administration and management over 55 million surface acres and 57 million acres of sub-surface minerals estates held in trust by the United States for American Indians, Indian Tribes, and Alaska Natives, and provides assistance to 566 federally-recognized tribal governments to help protect water, natural resources and land rights.

The **Bureau of Land Management** administers 247 million acres of Federal land and an additional 700 million acres of onshore Federal mineral estate, located primarily in 12 western states, including Alaska, characterized by grasslands, forests, deserts, coastline, and arctic tundra. The BLM sustains the ecological and economic health, diversity, and productivity of these public lands for the use and enjoyment of present and future generations.

Working in 17 states west of the Mississippi River, the **Bureau of Reclamation** manages 476 dams and 337 reservoirs covering more than 6.6 million acres associated with irrigation projects to protect local economies and preserve natural resources and ecosystems through the management and effective use of water resources.

The **U.S. Fish & Wildlife Service** conserves, protects and enhances fish, wildlife, and plants and their habitats and manages over 150 million acres within 561 National Wildlife Refuges, other refuge units, and 38 wetland management districts for the continuing benefit of the American people, providing primary trusteeship for migratory birds and over 2,000 threatened and endangered species.

The **National Park Service** preserves the natural and cultural resources and values of the 84 million acres of land and 4.5 million acres of oceans, lakes, and reservoirs of the 398 units of the national park system. The NPS seeks to conserve the scenery and the natural and historic objects and the wildlife of these special places for the enjoyment, education, and inspiration of current and future generations.

In addition to the five bureaus with primary trust resource management activities, the U.S. Geological Survey (USGS) conducts scientific research in ecosystems, climate and land use change, environmental health and water resources, and provides access to natural resource science to support effective decision making on how to best restore injured natural resources impacted by the release of oil or hazardous substances in the environment.

The DOI Office of the Secretary and the Office of the Solicitor also play key roles in making the Restoration Program a fully integrated Departmental program. The Office of the Solicitor provides legal advice, and the Office of Policy Analysis provides economic analytical expertise to the Program at both national policy and individual case management levels. The Office of Environmental Policy and Compliance provides a link to response and remedial activities associated with oil spills or chemical releases.

The Department, through its bureaus, conducts every damage assessment and restoration case in partnership with co-trustees at various levels (Federal, State, and tribal), and all restoration plans must undergo public review and be approved by affected State and Tribal governments. The Restoration Program serves as a model of collaboration in its day-to-day operations and partnerships that have been developed with Tribal, State, and other Federal co-trustees, as well as with non-governmental conservation organizations and industry.

Overview

The FY 2015 budget request for the Natural Resource Damage Assessment and Restoration Program totals $7,767,000, an increase of $1,504,000 over the 2014 enacted level. The requested increase supports the following program initiatives:

1. Restoration Support (+$.9 million and +3 FTE), is focused on providing additional staff and program capacity to increase the amount of restoration implementation across the country, and to ensure the effective utilization of the growing balance of restoration settlement funds in the DOI Restoration Fund. An increase in the number of dedicated program staff focused exclusively on implementing restoration will result in marked increases in the amount of acres and stream/shoreline miles being restored, along with attendant ecological and economic benefits for the American public.

2. Inland Oil Spill Preparedness ($1.0 million and +1 FTE), will allow the Department to develop the tools and contingency plans necessary to deal with potential inland oil spills. Conventional energy resources will continue to remain an important component as the Department moves forward in implementing the Department's *Powering Our Future and Responsible Use of Our Resources* initiative. Domestic oil and gas production and transportation are likely to continue at high, and potentially increasing, levels. New

forms of transportation entering into the industry (e.g., tank cars on high-speed rail and pipelines carrying tar sands/bitumen oil) pose new risks and challenges to spill planners and responders.

Administration Initiatives

America's Great Outdoors (AGO)

America's Great Outdoors fosters the intrinsic link between healthy economies and healthy landscapes to increase tourism and outdoor recreation in balance with preservation and conservation. This initiative features collaborative and community-driven efforts and outcome-focused investments focused on preserving and enhancing rural landscapes, urban parks and rivers, important ecosystems, cultural resources, and wildlife habitat. These activities incorporate the best available science, a landscape-level understanding, and stakeholder input to identify and share conservation priorities.

The AGO initiative seeks to empower all Americans to share in the responsibility to conserve, restore, and provide better access to our lands and waters in order to leave a healthy, vibrant outdoor legacy for generations to come. Funding for the initiative is broadly defined to capture programs that are key to attaining conservation goals. That includes funding to operate and maintain our public lands; expand and improve recreational opportunities at the state and local level; protect cultural resources; and conserve and restore land, water, and native species.

The Restoration Program has no discretionary appropriated funds that specifically tie to the AGO initiative. However, many of the projects, funded with permanent funds, accomplishes resource and recreational objectives that are consistent with the spirit and intent of the AGO initiative. A large percentage of DOI and its Federal, State, and tribal co-trustee partners' restoration actions and accomplishments are jointly accomplished using settlement funds recovered through the Restoration Program, often involve non-governmental conservation organizations, and are targeted toward the restoration, acquisition, or protection of public lands, creation of recreational opportunities, and the restoration of landscapes and trust species.

Administration's Management Agenda

The President's Management Agenda calls for cutting waste and implementing a government that is more responsive and open to the needs of the American people. The Department is actively engaged in supporting this agenda. The Restoration Program continues to meet the challenge of the *Campaign to Cut Waste*, which in 2015 maintains a focus on federal travel costs. Through the end of 2013, the Restoration Program and its components across the Department had met its Campaign to Cut Waste target goals. The continued and increased use of SharePoint collaboration tools and video conferencing when possible will continue to allow the program to minimize its travel costs in 2014 and 2015.

DOI Strategic Plan:

The FY 2014-2018 DOI Strategic Plan, provides a collection of mission objectives, goals, strategies and corresponding metrics that provide an integrated and focused approach for tracking performance across a wide range of DOI programs. While this Strategic Plan is the foundational structure for the description of program performance measurement and planning for the FY 2015 President's Budget, further details for achieving the Strategic Plan's goals are presented in the DOI Annual Performance Plan and Report (APP&R). Bureau and program specific plans for FY 2015 are fully consistent with the goals, outcomes, and measures described in the DOI Strategic Plan and related implementation information in the Annual Performance Plan and Report (APP&R).

Performance Summary

All activities within the Restoration Program (damage assessment, restoration support, in-land oil spill preparedness, and program management) support resource restoration either directly or as necessary steps on the road to restoration of injured natural resources under the trusteeship of the Department of the Interior. These restoration activities contribute towards Mission Area 1: Celebrating and Enhancing America's Great Outdoors / Goal No. 1 to Protect America's Landscapes and Goal No. 2 Protect America's Cultural and Heritage Resources. As is also the case with the Department's *America's Great Outdoors* initiative, the Program's restoration of injured natural resources includes activities as varied as partnerships to acquire high-value habitats; improve stewardship of Federal, State and tribal lands; and landscape-level conservation in key ecosystems.

In addition, the Program's damage assessment and restoration activities undertaken with tribal co-trustees support Mission Area 2 - Strengthening Tribal Nations and Insular Communities by working government-to-government as equal partners to restore injured tribal natural resources. The Program also seeks opportunities wherever possible to involve young people, either in hands-on restoration activities or outdoor classroom experiences, in support of the Youth Initiative as part of America's Great Outdoors.

As required by the Government Performance and Results Act of 1993, the Department recently published its Strategic Plan for Fiscal Years 2014 – 2018. This current Strategic Plan updated the prior plan (FY 2011 – 2016) and includes a simpler and more strategic set of goals and more finite and focused performance measures. NRDAR performance accomplishments (focusing on acres and miles of habitat restored) are first captured and reported by the individual bureaus implementing the restoration actions, and are included in those respective bureaus' reporting, often consolidated with other bureau-level restoration achievements. For purposes of reporting Restoration Program accomplishments, those same acres and stream miles are reported by the DOI bureau that is the lead agency in any given case. This budget request continues to report a summary of such on-the-ground restoration accomplishments. Performance measures reported here are not added to the Departmental strategic reporting in order to avoid potential issues of double-counting.

2015 Program Performance

In 2015, the Program expects to see measurable increases in the amount of restoration being achieved, notably through the Program's performance indicators of acres restored and stream/shoreline miles restored. A secondary measure monitoring the movement of settlement funds out of the Restoration Fund to DOI bureaus and involved co-trustees is expected to show increases in the amount of restoration funds released for on-the-ground implementation. These increases will result from the additional Restoration Support staff and resources contained in the 2015 budget request. The addition of new dedicated staff focused on supporting on-the-ground restoration will pay benefits within the first year.

The Program will continue to review, develop and implement guidance and regulatory reforms that directly address process improvements recommended over the past several years by field practitioners, co-trustees, and key stakeholders. The program will also continue to work closely with Federal, State, and tribal co-trustees and other interested parties to gather the most up to date information needed for guidance development. These improvements address four major policy areas: injury quantification, damage determination, analysis of restoration alternatives, and restoration implementation. Once implemented, the recommendations will lead to improved processes and tools to achieve long-term restoration goals that support the Department's mission and overall goal to protect the Nation's natural, cultural, and recreational resources.

In 2015, the Program will continue to focus its activities in support of trust resource restoration, and will, through the addition of additional Restoration Support staffing and resources, and the implementation of the program strategic plan recommendations, see increased restoration outputs and outcomes. Consistent with the Restoration Program's continued push to increase restoration staffing and capacity, in order to accomplish more restoration, and thus reflecting significant anticipated gains in acres and stream/shoreline miles restored, the Fiscal Year 2015 planned performance targets include the restoration of 100,000 acres and 250 stream or shoreline miles, increases of 77,500 acres (+344%) and 70 stream/shoreline miles (+39%), respectively over outdated FY 2014 strategic plan target goals. The significant increases in the number of acres and stream/shoreline miles to be restored in 2015 is a reflection of prior years actual performance, and is more in line with updated program expectations following the implementation of the Program's strategic plan. Attainment of these goals will be accomplished by the Department and its co-trustees through the use of funds or in-kind services received in settlement of damage claims with responsible parties.

A secondary performance indicator used by the Program is monitoring the amount of funds disbursed from the Restoration Fund to the bureaus and co-trustees to implement on-the-ground restoration projects. In Fiscal Year 2013, the Restoration Program released $59.4 million to trustee agencies for restoration activities. To date, through the first five months of Fiscal Year 2014, the program has released nearly $15 million for restoration.

Restoration program performance measures and accomplishments in all four program activities (Damage Assessment, Restoration Support, In-land Oil Spill Preparedness, and Program Management) are singularly focused on one goal, the increased restoration of acres and stream/shoreline miles. Such restoration creates or protects habitat for injured biological communities to recuperate, thrive, and flourish. Programmatic performance accomplishments at the activity level are but a step leading to the implementation of restoration actions. Within the Damage Assessment activity, data is collected annually on all Departmentally-funded cases, which enables the Program to monitor the progress of cases through the assessment process to settlement, using measures such as number of cases reaching various milestones, numbers of cooperative assessments with industry, and number of cases settled. In 2015, the Program will continue to work with the USGS on a restoration science initiative to develop protocols and metrics to better measure the ecological outcomes of restoration activities, including measures relating to carbon capture and climate change.

The Restoration Program's performance goals reflect continued progress funded with monies and in-kind actions recovered in settlement from responsible parties, and not appropriated funds. Appropriated discretionary funds are used to fund damage assessments, administer the program, conduct in-land oil spill preparedness, and provide technical support. Recent successful settlement of natural resource damage claims in 2013 has contributed to the continuing high balance of the Restoration Fund. Settlement of cases such as the St. Lawrence River, NY site ($10.0 million), Coeur d'Alene Basin, ID ($8.3 million), the M/V Cape Flattery grounding, HI ($5.9 million) and the Industri-plex Superfund Site, MA ($4.2 million) have added almost $46 million earmarked for site-specific restoration to the fund in 2013. As of the end of February 2014, there was $434 million in joint and shared settlement funds in the DOI Restoration Fund that are dedicated for restoration activities that will allow the program to continue moving forward towards its long term restoration goals in concert with its co-trustee partners.

Restoration accomplishments in acres and stream/shoreline miles restored often fluctuate from year-to-year, the result of a complex process in which numerous trustee councils across the Nation are moving forward in identifying specific opportunities for restoration consistent with approved restoration plans, but which generally cannot be scheduled or readily anticipated on a site-specific basis. The year-to-year variability in performance shown on the following table reflects the pace of restoration which is greatly influenced by factors outside the Department's control, such as finding cooperative landowners or willing sellers.

There are a number of efforts currently underway that will help the Restoration Program meet its performance goals for 2015. During 2014, working with its Executive Board, the Program will complete an independent program evaluation, focusing on how the Program can best align its resources and activities to achieve additional support to accelerate the completion of restoration projects. Continued program maturity and an unrelenting focus on achieving restoration will provide the impetus for case teams in getting restoration projects underway sooner. The FY 2015 proposed increase for the Restoration Support activity will provide additional, dedicated restoration tools and services such as contracting, realty support, legal support, restoration planning, project management, and engineering support to be provided by the Restoration Support Unit, giving case teams an expanding set of tools for restoration implementation.

The increasingly common use of cooperative assessments is expected to continue, thus minimizing the chance of adversarial confrontations with responsible parties, and thus allowing case teams to move more quickly to settlement and restoration. In addition, the Office is working with the bureaus to continue to enhance internal and external restoration partnerships and to make greater use of existing watershed, landscape, or flyway scale restoration plans to jumpstart NRD restoration implementation where appropriate. In the longer term, regulatory, policy and operational improvements arising from practitioner, co-trustee, and stakeholder recommendations will lead to better, more efficient damage assessments, which will lead to quicker and more effective restorations, positioning the Restoration Program to achieve its long-term strategic plan goals.

Cost information, including unit costs, in the context of performance measurement is of limited value within the Restoration Program, due to the wide variability of possible restoration solutions that might be implemented and the multi-year implementation time-frames they often entail. Every restoration implemented is unique, from the resource injury being addressed, to the ecological, biological, and engineering aspects involved, and the number and roles of other involved co-trustees, partners, and responsible parties. The wide range of possible but generally not comparable restoration actions is best exemplified in the restoration success stories found in the Restoration Support section.

The bureaus will continue to collect, validate, and verify the performance data before reporting to the Program. In addition, the Program Office will continue to track internally the progress of cases from start to finish using measures such as increased numbers of restoration plans drafted, finalized, and in stages of implementation; increased numbers of restorations completed; increased numbers of cooperative assessments with industry; and increased funding leveraged from restoration partnerships.

Mission Area 1: Provide natural and cultural resource protection and experiences

Goal #1: Protect America's Landscapes

Strategic Objective Metrics Strategic Plan Measure / Efficiency or other Bureau-specific Measure	2010 Actual	2011 Actual	2012 Actual	2013 Plan	2013 Actual	2014 Plan	2015 Request
Strategy #1: Improve land and water health by restoring wetlands and uplands that support trust natural resources that have been injured by oil spills or releases of hazardous substances							
Number of acres restored or enhanced to achieve desired habitat conditions to support trust species conservation	68,834	87,709	97,813	18,750	122,360	22,500	100,000
Comments: Year to year variability is expected based on variability of timing and settlement amounts.							
Contributing Programs: NRDAR, FWS Environmental Contaminants, NPS, BIA, BLM, BOR, USGS, SOL, OS/Policy Analysis, other Federal, State, and tribal co-trustees							
Strategy #2: Improve land and water health by restoring riparian, stream, and shoreline areas that support trust natural resources that have been injured by oil spills or releases of hazardous substances							
Number of stream or shoreline miles restored or enhanced to achieve desired habitat conditions to support trust species conservation	377	401	409	165	332	180	250
Comments: Year to year variability is expected based on variability of timing and settlement amounts.							
Contributing Programs: NRDAR, FWS Environmental Contaminants, NPS, BIA, BLM, BOR, USGS, SOL, OS/Policy Analysis, other Federal, State, and tribal co-trustees							

Note: The actual and planned acres and miles presented in this table are included among the performance results and targets presented in the Performance Budgets of the bureaus. As such, in order to avoid double-counting, these acres and miles are not included in the Department's aggregate results calculations or performance projections.

The DOI Office of Restoration and Damage Assessment (ORDA) manages the Restoration Program, and currently consists of ten (10) direct FTE. They are the Office Director and nine staff: the Deputy Office Director for Restoration, the Assistant Office Director for Operations, the Budget Officer/Restoration Fund Manager, and three program operations staff located in its Washington, DC headquarters, as well as three staff Restoration Support specialists located in Denver, Colorado. The following organization chart goes beyond the small number of people in the Program Management Office and reflects the integrated management structure of the Program as a whole, with the inter-related components of six bureaus, the Office of the Solicitor, and two offices within the Office of the Secretary.

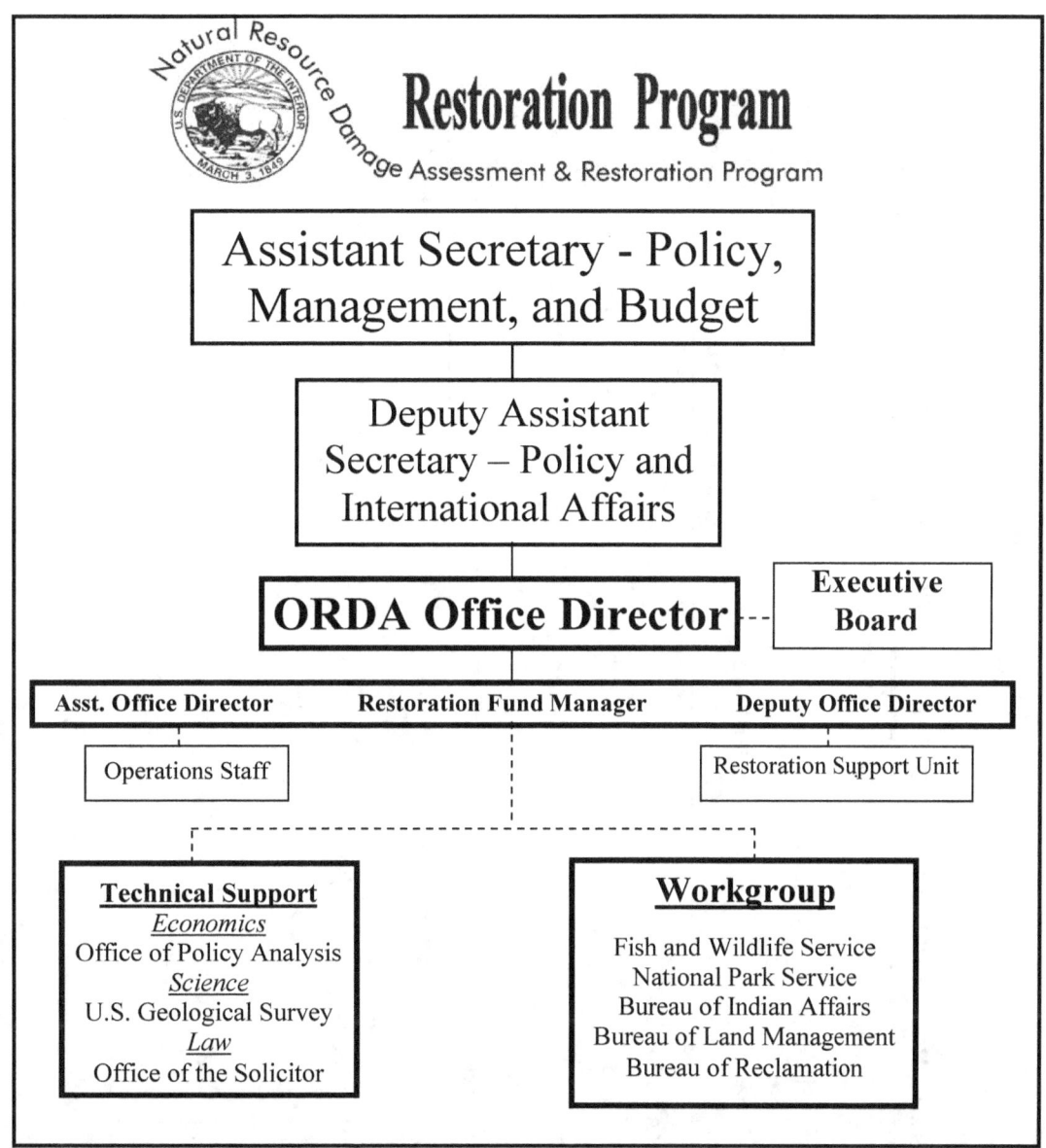

The Restoration Program reports to the Deputy Assistant Secretary – Policy and International Affairs, under the Assistant Secretary - Policy, Management, and Budget (AS-PMB). There is also a "Restoration Executive Board" representative at the assistant director level for BIA, BLM, BOR, FWS and NPS; a Deputy Associate Solicitor, and the Director of the Office of Environmental Policy and Compliance. The Restoration Executive Board is responsible for overseeing policy direction and approving allocation of resources.

Summary of Requirements Table
(Dollars in Thousands)

Appropriation: Natural Resource Damage Assessment and Restoration

Comparison by Activity / Subactivity

Activity	2013 Actual		2014 Enacted		Fixed Costs (+/-)		Program Changes (+/-)		2015 Budget Request		Inc. (+)/ Dec(-) from 2014 Enacted	
	FTE	Amount	FTE	Amount	FTE	Amount	FTE	Amount	FTE	Amount	FTE	Amount
APPROPRIATED FUNDS												
Damage Assessments	0	3,150	0	3,157	0	+17	0	-674	0	2,500	0	-657
Restoration Support	2	1,159	3	1,171	0	+4	+3	+900	6	2,075	+3	+904
Oil Spill Preparedness	0	0	0	0	0	0	+1	+1,000	1	1,000	+1	+1,000
Program Management	7	1,931	7	1,935	0	+18	0	+239	7	2,192	0	+257
Total, Appropriation	9	6,240	10	6,263	0	+39	+4	+1,465	14	7,767	+4	+1,504
PERMANENT FUNDS (RECEIPTS)												
Damage Assessments		22,635		13,324		0		+576		13,900		+576
Restoration												
[Prince William Sound Restoration]		6,206		6,000		0		0		6,000		0
[Other Restoration]		39,586		60,000		0		0		60,000		0
Program Management		75		100		0		0		100		0
Subtotal, Gross Receipts	0	68,502	0	79,424	0	0	0	+576	0	80,000	0	+576
Transfers Out		-4,153		-6,000		0		0		-6,000		0
Total, Net Receipts		64,349		73,424		0		+576		74,000		+576

Natural Resource Damage Assessment and Restoration Program

Justification of Fixed Costs and Internal Realignments
(Dollars In Thousands)

Other Fixed Cost Changes and Projections	2014 Total	2014 to 2015 Change
Change in Number of Paid Days	-	+0

This column reflects changes in pay associated with the change in the number of paid days between 2014 and 2015. In years where there is no change in paid days, the salary impact will be zero.

Pay Raise	-	+59

The change reflects the salary impact of the 1% programmed pay raise.

Employer Share of Federal Health Benefit Plans	+3	+4

The change reflects expected increases in employer's share of Federal Health Benefit Plans.

Departmental Working Capital Fund	120	-24

The change reflects expected changes in the charges for centrally billed Department services and other services through the Working Capital Fund. These charges are displayed in the Budget Justification for Department Management.

Rental Payments	106	+0

The adjustment is for changes in the costs payable to General Services Administration (GSA) and others resulting from changes in rates for office and non-office space as estimated by GSA, as well as the rental costs of other currently occupied space. These costs include building security; in the case of GSA space, these are paid to Department of Homeland Security (DHS). Costs of mandatory office relocations, i.e. relocations in cases where due to external events there is no alternative but to vacate the currently occupied space, are also included.

Natural Resource Damage Assessment and Restoration Program

Appropriations Language

NATURAL RESOURCE DAMAGE ASSESSMENT FUND

To conduct natural resource damage assessment, restoration activities, and onshore oil spill preparedness by the Department of the Interior necessary to carry out the provisions of the Comprehensive Environmental Response, Compensation, and Liability Act (42 U.S.C. 9601 et seq.), the Federal Water Pollution Control Act (33 U.S.C. 1251 et seq.), the Oil Pollution Act of 1990 (33 U.S.C. 2701 et seq.), and Public Law 101-337 (16 U.S.C. 19jj et seq.), [$6,263,000] *$7,767,000*, to remain available until expended. *(Department of the Interior, Environment, and Related Agencies Appropriations Act, 2014.)*

Authorizing Statutes:

Comprehensive Environmental Response, Compensation, and Liability Act, as amended, *(42 U.S.C 9601 et seq.).* Section 106 of the Act authorizes the President to clean up hazardous substance sites directly, or obtain cleanup by a responsible party through enforcement actions. Trustees for natural resources may assess and recover damages for injury to natural resources from releases of hazardous substances and use the damages for restoration, replacement or acquisition of equivalent natural resources. Provides permanent authorization to appropriate receipts from responsible parties.

Federal Water Pollution Control Act (Clean Water Act), as amended, *(33 U.S.C. 1251-1387).* Authorizes trustees for natural resources to assess and recover damages for injuries to natural resources resulting from the discharge of oil into or upon the navigable waters of the United States, adjoining shorelines, the waters of the contiguous zone, or in connection with activities under the *Outer Continental Shelf Lands Act* or the *Deepwater Port Act of 1974*, or which may affect natural resources belonging to, appertaining to, or under the exclusive management authority of the United States.

Oil Pollution Act of 1990, (33 U.S.C. 2701 et seq.) Amends the *Federal Water Pollution Control Act*, and authorizes trustee(s) of natural resources to present a claim for and to recover damages for injuries to natural resources from each responsible party for a vessel or facility from which oil is discharged, or which poses a substantial threat of discharge of oil, into or upon the navigable waters or adjoining shorelines or the exclusive zone.

National Park System Resource Protection Act (P.L. 101-337) (16 U.S.C. 19jj). Provides that response costs and damages recovered under it or amounts recovered under any statute as a result of damage to any Federal resource within a unit of the National Park System shall be retained and used for response costs, damage assessments, restoration, and replacements. Liability for damages under this Act is in addition to any other liability that may arise under other statutes.

Interior and Related Agencies Appropriation Act, 1992 (P.L. 102-154). Provides permanent authorization for receipts for damage assessment and restoration activities to be available without further appropriation until expended.

Dire Emergency Supplemental Appropriations for Fiscal Year 1992 (P.L. 102-229). Provides that the Fund's receipts are authorized to be invested and available until expended. Also provides that amounts received by United States in settlement of *U.S. v Exxon Corp. et al.* in FY 1992 and thereafter be deposited into the Fund.

Interior and Related Agencies Appropriation Act, 1998 (P.L. 104-134). Provides authority to make transfers of settlement funds to other federal trustees and payments to non-federal trustees.

ACTIVITY: DAMAGE ASSESSMENT

Representatives of the U.S. Fish and Wildlife Service and Duke Energy collect samples of coal ash along the banks of the Dan River in southern Virginia. A February 2014 break in a storm water pipe released an estimated 80,000 tons of coal ash, mixed with 27 million gallons of water, into the river. (Photo credit - Steve Alexander, FWS)

Appropriation: Natural Resource Damage Assessment		2014 Enacted	Fixed Costs	Internal Transfers (+/-)	Program Changes (+/-)	2015 Request
Activity: Damage Assessment	$000	3,157	+17	0	-674	2,500
	FTE	0	0	0	0	0

Justification of 2015 Program Change:

Damage Assessment (-$674,000 / 0 FTE) – The 2015 budget request for the Damage Assessments activity is $2,500,000, a reduction of $674,000 from the 2014 enacted level. The decrease to the Damage Assessment activity will be offset with funds recovered (previously-funded damage assessment costs) from settled cases deposited into the permanent account. A number of recent settlements in previously-funded damage assessment cases have resulted in the recovery of past assessment costs that will be used to fund selected damage assessment cases going forward, in lieu of discretionary appropriated damage assessment funds. The total funding available for damage assessment cases will remain level and the program's overall capacity to conduct damage assessment activities is not expected to change.

Activity Overview:

Damage assessment activities are the critical first step taken by the Department on the long journey to achieving restoration of natural resources injured through the release of oil or hazardous substances. The source and magnitude of injury must first be identified, investigated, and thoroughly understood if the subsequent restoration is to be effective. Through the damage assessment process, physical and scientific evidence of natural resource injury is documented, which then forms the basis for the Department's claim for appropriate compensation (or in-kind services) to compensate the American public for the loss and use of those injured resources. The resulting restoration settlements allow the Restoration Program to then restore those injured trust resources, in concert with other affected natural resource trustee agencies. Damage assessment activities support the Department's performance outcome goals of protecting the Nation's natural and cultural resources. Information regarding the nature, pathway, and magnitude of the injury, and the means by which they are determined, also help establish the focus of the subsequent restoration plans and influence the determination of when those goals have been successfully reached.

Damage assessment cases are conducted by one or more of the five resource management bureaus within the Department: (Fish and Wildlife Service; National Park Service; Bureau of Land Management; Bureau of Indian Affairs, and Bureau of Reclamation). All FTE involved in supporting this activity are allocation FTE, located in the Departmental bureaus, there are no direct FTE within the Program Office. Economic analytical support is provided by the Office of Policy Analysis. Scientific and technical analysis and support is provided by the U.S. Geological Survey. And, legal counsel is provided by the Office of the Solicitor. In nearly all cases, assessment activities are carried out in partnership with other affected Federal, State, and/or tribal co-trustees. These partnerships have proven advantageous for all involved, as cooperation, consultation and collaboration amongst the trustees facilitates addressing overlapping areas of trustee concern, and consolidates those concerns into a single case. Trustees can also share data, achieve economies of scale, avoid duplication of effort and minimize administrative burdens and expenses. Responsible parties also benefit, as they are able to address all trustee concerns in a single, unified case.

The Restoration Program continues to make progress in conducting many of its damage assessment cases on a cooperative basis with responsible parties. As a matter of practice, responsible parties are invited to participate in the development of assessment and restoration plans. The Department has been involved in forty-nine cooperative assessments across the nation, where the responsible parties have elected to participate in the damage assessment process, and provide input into the selection of various injury studies and contribute advance funds or reimburse Interior for its assessment activities prior to settlement. In Fiscal Year 2013, over $34 million in advanced and/or reimbursed cooperative assessment funding was received from cooperating responsible parties for DOI's assessment activities at thirteen sites, including $30.3 million from BP related to the Deepwater Horizon Oil Spill in the Gulf of Mexico. This continuously-focused effort to use cooperative Funding and Participation Agreements with responsible parties to the greatest extent possible allows the Department to stretch its discretionary appropriated and recovered assessment funds further, thus funding additional cases it might not otherwise fund.

Selection of damage assessment projects is accomplished on an annual basis through an extensive internal proposal and screening process that assures that only the highest priority cases are funded. Significant consideration is given to those damage assessment cases that have the potential to address and support Administration or Secretarial priorities and initiatives, such as *America's Great Outdoors*. Criteria for selecting initial projects are based upon a case's likelihood of success in achieving restoration, either through negotiated restoration settlements or through successful litigation where necessary. Cases must demonstrate sufficient technical, legal, and administrative merit focused on the purpose of achieving restoration.

The Restoration Program's project selection process is designed to:

- Be inclusive of all natural resources under Interior trusteeship and trustee roles;
- Provide a process that encourages thorough planning and ultimately, strong opportunities for restoration success;
- Provide a process that evaluates both the objective and subjective aspects of individual cases; and
- Fund cases that have demonstrated sufficient levels of technical and legal merit, trustee organization, and case readiness.

DOI bureaus are also required to coordinate their planning and operational efforts into a single project proposal, thus promoting inter-Departmental efficiencies and eliminating duplication of effort. Bureau and DOI office capabilities are used to augment and complement each other, as opposed to building redundant program capabilities in multiple bureaus.

Once projects are funded, the Restoration Program makes use of project-level performance information to inform and guide future funding decisions. The Restoration Program relies on performance data collected from ongoing cases that document the attainment of specific chronological milestones (trustee MOU, assessment plan development, injury determination and quantification, preliminary estimate of damages, etc.) in the multi-year process toward settlement. Funding decisions were weighted in favor of those cases that continue to show progress along the damage assessment continuum towards settlement and eventual restoration. Cases that stall or fail to progress are considered a lesser priority, and are given direction to make course corrections at a stable or reduced funding level. Course corrections must be made before additional funding is made available for addressing future milestones. For example, a case team may be directed to finalize necessary procedural products such as a publicly-announced assessment plan before beginning its scientific studies. The use of such project-level performance data lends itself to helping the Restoration Program better manage its workload by having a clearer sense of when damage assessment cases are near completion and opportunities for new starts emerge.

In addition to project milestone reporting, financial obligation data is monitored at the aggregate (DOI), bureau, and project levels across all involved bureaus. This obligation data and carryover balances are factors considered in the annual project funding decision process. Further, unobligated balances on all damage assessment projects are closely monitored from inception through settlement, at which time all unused or unneeded funds are identified, pulled back and re-allocated to other high-priority damage assessment projects. In some instances and under certain circumstances, case teams have been directed to or have voluntarily returned project funds from ongoing projects so that they can be re-allocated to other projects and needs.

The program requires its case teams to document their respective assessment costs and attempts to recover those costs from the potentially responsible parties when negotiating settlement agreements. Over the past three fiscal year funding cycles (2012 – 2014), the Program has utilized an average of $2.1 million annually in damage assessment funds recovered in settlement, in combination with its annual discretionary appropriations in order to continue ongoing damage assessment work at current sites or to initiate new cases.

2015 Activity Performance

In 2015, the program will continue to utilize a mix of discretionary appropriations, recovered past assessment costs from recent settlements and/or returned funds from completed assessments, as well as advanced funds from cooperative responsible parties to meet its damage assessment workload requirements. The combined appropriated and recovered funds will support new or ongoing damage assessment efforts at approximately 35 sites, maintaining the program's damage assessment capability at current levels. This level of funding will support new feasibility studies, initiation of assessments at new sites where warranted, as well as providing continued funding for ongoing cases towards completion and settlement. In most years, the program anticipates that the annual project proposals received from the field will exceed the amount of available funding, thus leading the program to carefully scrutinize, select, and fund those cases best focused on Administration and Secretarial priorities, and best organized and prepared to advance towards settlement. The program will also continue its focus on the use of cooperative assessments, and pursue advance funding agreements with potentially responsible parties wherever and whenever possible. Money provided under these funding agreements will expand program coverage by allowing other damage assessment cases to utilize the appropriated and recovered/returned assessment funds. In addition, the program will continue to refine its milestone reporting process and use that performance data to enhance management of its damage assessment workload. Lastly, the Program shall continue its efforts to work closely with other trustee partners to jointly identify future workload, those new sites and incidents requiring an assessment of natural resource injury

The Program's current damage assessment project caseload through 2014 totals 61 ongoing cases (including feasibility studies), and are among those depicted on the map and table on the following pages.

Damage Assessment and Restoration Sites
Funded by the Department of the Interior Restoration Fund

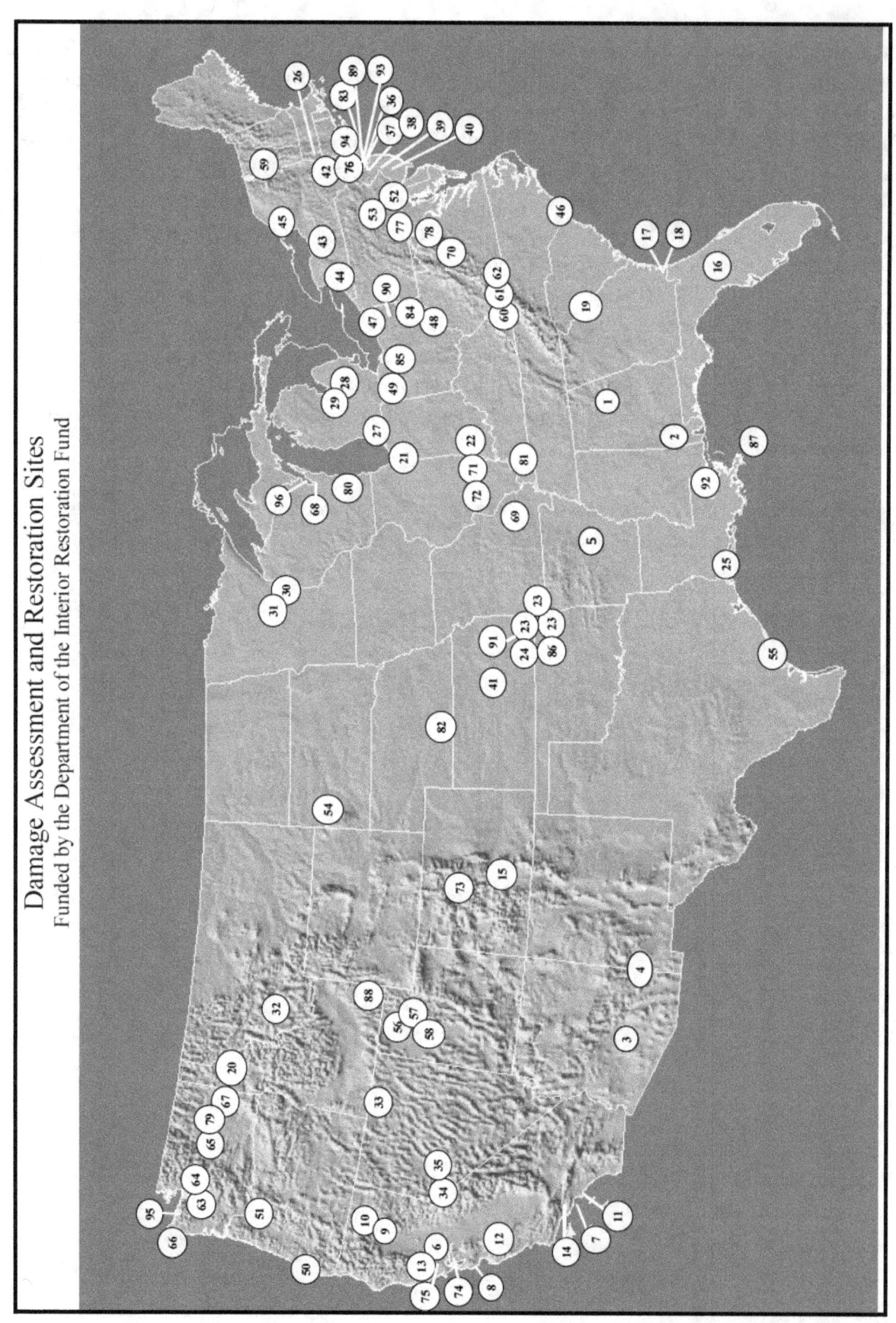

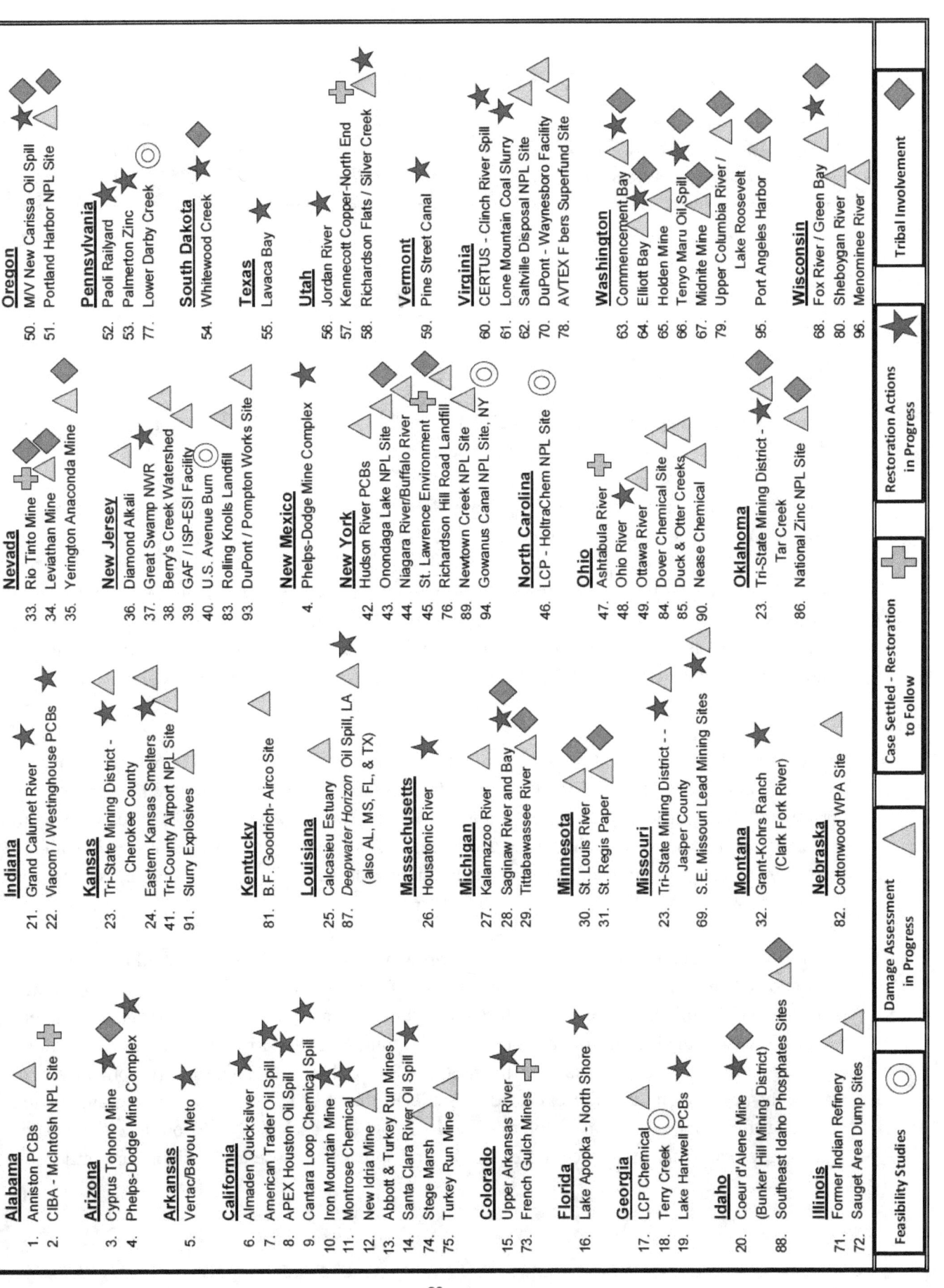

Alabama
1. Anniston PCBs
2. CIBA - McIntosh NPL Site

Arizona
3. Cyprus Tohono Mine
4. Phelps-Dodge Mine Complex

Arkansas
5. Vertac/Bayou Meto

California
6. Almaden Quicksilver
7. American Trader Oil Spill
8. APEX Houston Oil Spill
9. Cantara Loop Chemical Spill
10. Iron Mountain Mine
11. Montrose Chemical
12. New Idria Mine
13. Abbott & Turkey Run Mines
74. Santa Clara River Oil Spill
14. Stege Marsh
75. Turkey Run Mine

Colorado
15. Upper Arkansas River
73. French Gulch Mines

Florida
16. Lake Apopka - North Shore

Georgia
17. LCP Chemical
18. Terry Creek
19. Lake Hartwell PCBs

Idaho
20. Coeur d'Alene Mine (Bunker Hill Mining District)
88. Southeast Idaho Phosphates Sites

Illinois
71. Former Indian Refinery
72. Sauget Area Dump Sites

Indiana
21. Grand Calumet River
22. Viacom / Westinghouse PCBs

Kansas
23. Tri-State Mining District - Cherokee County
24. Eastern Kansas Smelters
41. Tri-County Airport NPL Site
91. Slurry Explosives

Kentucky
81. B.F. Goodrich- Airco Site

Louisiana
25. Calcasieu Estuary
87. Deepwater Horizon Oil Spill, LA (also AL, MS, FL, & TX)

Massachusetts
26. Housatonic River

Michigan
27. Kalamazoo River
28. Saginaw River and Bay
29. Tittabawassee River

Minnesota
30. St. Louis River
31. St. Regis Paper

Missouri
23. Tri-State Mining District -- Jasper County
69. S.E. Missouri Lead Mining Sites

Montana
32. Grant-Kohrs Ranch (Clark Fork River)

Nebraska
82. Cottonwood WPA Site

Nevada
33. Rio Tinto Mine
34. Leviathan Mine
35. Yerington Anaconda Mine

New Jersey
36. Diamond Alkali
37. Great Swamp NWR
38. Berry's Creek Watershed
39. GAF / ISP-ESI Facility
40. U.S. Avenue Burn
83. Rolling Knolls Landfill
93. DuPont / Pompton Works Site

New Mexico
4. Phelps-Dodge Mine Complex

New York
42. Hudson River PCBs
43. Onondaga Lake NPL Site
44. Niagara River/Buffalo River
45. St. Lawrence Environment
76. Richardson Hill Road Landfill
89. Newtown Creek NPL Site
94. Gowanus Canal NPL Site, NY

North Carolina
46. LCP - HoltraChem NPL Site

Ohio
47. Ashtabula River
48. Ohio River
49. Ottawa River
84. Dover Chemical Site
85. Duck & Otter Creeks
90. Nease Chemical

Oklahoma
23. Tri-State Mining District - Tar Creek
86. National Zinc NPL Site

Oregon
50. M/V New Carissa Oil Spill
51. Portland Harbor NPL Site

Pennsylvania
52. Paoli Railyard
53. Palmerton Zinc
77. Lower Darby Creek

South Dakota
54. Whitewood Creek

Texas
55. Lavaca Bay

Utah
56. Jordan River
57. Kennecott Copper-North End
58. Richardson Flats / Silver Creek

Vermont
59. Pine Street Canal

Virginia
60. CERTUS - Clinch River Spill
61. Lone Mountain Coal Slurry
62. Saltville Disposal NPL Site
70. DuPont - Waynesboro Facility
78. AVTEX F bers Superfund Site

Washington
63. Commencement Bay
64. Elliott Bay
65. Holden Mine
66. Tenyo Maru Oil Spill
67. Midnite Mine
79. Upper Columbia River / Lake Roosevelt
95. Port Angeles Harbor

Wisconsin
68. Fox River / Green Bay
80. Sheboygan River
96. Menominee River

Feasibility Studies

Damage Assessment in Progress

Case Settled - Restoration to Follow

Restoration Actions in Progress

Tribal Involvement

ACTIVITY: RESTORATION SUPPORT

Appropriation: Natural Resource Damage Assessment		2014 Enacted	Fixed Costs	Internal Transfers (+/-)	Program Changes (+/-)	2015 Request
Activity: Restoration Support	$000	1,171	+4	0	+900	2,075
	FTE	3	0	0	+3	6

Justification of 2015 Program Changes:

Restoration Support (+$900,000 / +3 FTE) - The 2015 budget request for Restoration Support is $2,075,000 and 6 direct FTE, a program increase of $900,000 and 3 direct FTE from the 2014 enacted level. The requested increase for Restoration Support in 2015 will enable the Department to provide additional staff to the Program's Restoration Support Unit (RSU) to increase our ability to implement restoration projects.

During 2014, working with its restoration partners, the Department has identified specific skill shortages that have slowed the progress toward restoration project completions. The requested increase will be used to provide skills such as legal and contracting support, as well as dedicated restoration specialists to those projects where these additional skills would be most effectively used.

Initially, the RSU staff will look to jump-start restoration actions at sites where recovered settlement funds have sat idle for more than three years, as well as focus their efforts on the largest settlements held in the Restoration Fund. In addition, they will look for cases with small settlement dollars in which there is a geographic connection or common link to the injured resources in order to combine these settlement amounts and achieve a larger, regional restoration project that will more fully restore injured resources.

The DOI Restoration Fund continues to hold a growing balance of funds recovered in settlements of previous damage assessment cases. Over the last four years, the Fund has received an average of nearly $135 million per year in restoration settlements and cooperative damage assessment funds, increasing the balance of funds two-fold. A number of long-running damage assessment cases have recently settled, many with multi-million dollar settlements. Still others are in settlement negotiations and are expected to settle in the next few years, including anticipated additional funds for ecological restoration from Restore Act activities and from a settlement for natural resource injury in the Deepwater Horizon oil spill when those injury claims are settled.

Despite significant gains in restoration outcomes in 2012 and 2013, the Department's current Restoration Program infrastructure and restoration-focused staffing has not been able to keep pace with this explosive growth in settlement funds. Current restoration staffing is inadequate, and additional staffing is needed to implement settlement-funded restoration.

While bureau-staffed case teams can and do use settlement funds for staff time and to implement on-the-ground restoration projects, often there are insufficient full-time dedicated restoration support personnel necessary to successfully plan and implement restoration plans. For any given settlement, the parties responsible for the spill or release of hazardous substances into the environment are responsible for restoring injured natural resources for that specific site. However, they bear no responsibility for maintaining the necessary cadre of restoration specialists needed to successfully staff and support a wide range of restoration support activities across the nation.

Currently, the Restoration Support Unit (RSU) provides a wide suite of restoration support services to case teams and trustee councils across the Nation, including the following:

- Restoration planning, including development of the required restoration plan which must be publicly reviewed;
- Restoration science technical support;
- National Environmental Policy Act (NEPA) compliance support;
- Engineering Support (General engineering, hydrology, fluvial geomorphology, construction engineering, value engineering and cost estimation);
- Project management planning and support, and
- Liaison with other restoration programs and services across the spectrum (government/contractor/non-profits/local organizations)

With the requested increase, the RSU will offer dedicated staff with necessary skill sets and expertise required to write restoration plans and implement restoration projects. These skills sets are not widely available to case teams and this shortage has been identified by field practitioners as an impediment to timely restoration. Further, these skill sets would reflect the training and expertise that is necessary for the cooperative nature of restoration, which differs from the skill set suited for the often adversarial setting of damage assessments and NRDA claim resolution. In addition, the requested 2015 increase will provide for additional staff (as allocation FTE) assigned to the RSU that would provide additional restoration support services, including:

- Legal Support, through the Office of the Solicitor to address various restoration-related legal issues, review documents, and provide counsel to case teams nationwide,

- Contract Specialists, located within a bureau to provide dedicated NRDAR support with appropriate warrant level for grants, cooperative agreements, and contracts.

By providing additional dedicated, readily-available restoration support staff, tools, and services, the RSU will seek to supplement and complement the efforts of the bureau-level case teams, who already have the important day-to-day operational and working relationships with other involved co-trustee agencies.

The potential benefits associated with this budget request are significant, for both injured natural resources and the American public. With nearly a half billion dollars in settlement funds currently residing in the DOI Restoration Fund, and more settlements on the horizon, moving forward deliberately and strategically in the implementation of restoration actions at dozens of sites nationwide will produce benefits, both ecologically and economically.

Activity Overview:

The restoration of injured natural resources is the sole reason for the existence of the Department's natural resource damage assessment and restoration program. Every action the Restoration Program undertakes is done with the end goal of restoration in mind. Upon the successful conclusion of a natural resource injury assessment and upon achieving settlement with the responsible parties, DOI bureaus working in partnership with other affected State, Federal, tribal and/or foreign co-trustees, use settlement funds to carry out restoration activities. Under the Restoration Support activity, the Program continues its coordinated effort to focus greater attention on restoration activities and to expedite the expenditure of settlement funds to develop and implement restoration plans. The program's RSU staff, upon request, provides engineering and ecological/biological support to the Department's case managers/teams, as well as assistance with meeting various legal and regulatory compliance requirements (such as NEPA compliance), identifying possible partnering opportunities, and drafting appropriate documents. In addition, the Program continues to work with the U.S. Geological Survey in the field of restoration ecology to develop monitoring protocols to better measure the success and impacts of restoration efforts.

In meeting the statutory and regulatory requirements to restore, replace, or acquire the equivalent of the natural resources that were injured by the release of oil or hazardous materials, these restoration activities encompass a wide variety of projects that support the Department's mission of protecting natural and cultural resources. By working with the co-trustees on restoration activities, the Program is able to focus restoration actions which often support and contribute to the *America's Great Outdoors* initiative through ecological restoration, land acquisition and/or protection. Some restoration projects also provide indirect support to the Secretary's *Strengthening Tribal Nations* initiative via Tribal co-trustee interactions and restoration projects benefitting tribal communities. In addition, many projects engage youth in restoration activities and outdoor classrooms. These activities include multiple sites in high priority landscapes such as the Great Lakes, the California Bay/Delta, Chesapeake Bay, and the Gulf of Mexico; land acquisition for several National Wildlife Refuges and numerous State and local parks; protection and reintroduction of threatened and endangered species helping lead to their eventual recovery; and protection and restoration of essential habitat for migratory birds and fish.

The DOI Restoration Program uses both current discretionary appropriations along with permanent mandatory funding to achieve its restoration program mission needs as follows:

- **Current Funding** – Current discretionary funds are used to support the existing RSU staff, and to support ecological restoration science research conducted by USGS.
- **Permanent (mandatory) Funding** – Consists of all incoming funds paid by responsible parties. Nearly ninety percent of all such funds received and interest currently in the Restoration Fund from settled damage assessment cases are designated as joint restoration funds, and can be used only for the Trustee's restoration planning, implementation (including land acquisition), oversight, and monitoring of implemented restoration actions at a specific site or related to a specific settlement, and only after the development and issuance of an publicly-reviewed restoration plan. The use of such settlement funds provides real value to the American public, as injured natural resources and services are restored by, or at the expense of the responsible party, and not the taxpaying public.

Other Available Restoration Resources (Dollars in $000)		
	2013	**2014**
Settlement funds currently held in DOI Restoration Fund (estimate)	$485,811	$470,000
Settlement funds in various court registry accounts (estimate)	$100,000	$100,000

In addition to settlement funds deposited into the DOI Restoration Fund, the Department is party to other natural resource damage settlements where settlement funds are deposited into a Court Registry or some other account selected by the Trustees. Additionally, there are a number of settlements where the responsible parties have agreed to undertake or implement the restoration actions, with trustee agencies providing oversight to ensure compliance with the terms of the settlement and adherence to the approved and publicly-reviewed restoration plan. Once fully implemented, the restoration actions are then subject to long-term monitoring by the trustees to ensure they have been effective and have met the goals and intent of the restoration plans.

All restoration activities are focused on restoring those resources and the services they provide back to the baseline level they would have had in the absence of the spill or release of hazardous substances. This encompasses preserving and maintaining the lands, waters, and wildlife of the Nation's public lands, embodied in wildlife refuges, national parks, and BLM lands as well as recovering trust resources that are on private or tribal lands. Results are achieved through DOI-administered programs and through partnership efforts and in collaboration with others in and out of government. These efforts are as widely varied as the trust resources the Department manages. Examples of these activities include:

- Restoration of nesting habitat for migratory birds;
- Re-introduction and re-establishment of endangered species;
- Acquisition of property that is added to the National Wildlife Refuge System or the lands managed by state, tribal, or local governments;
- In-stream and riparian habitat improvement to improve aquatic communities, fisheries, or fish passage;
- Control or removal of invasive species of plants and animals and re-establishment of native flora and fauna, and
- Providing recreational opportunities or protecting cultural uses and activities that flow from trust resources.

The Office of Restoration and Damage Assessment (Program Office) continues to work at the national program level to foster increased on-the-ground restoration results among the bureaus. To further this effort, the Restoration Program (along with involved DOI bureaus) has initiated a detailed programmatic evaluation to examine its program infrastructure, operations, and staffing on a Department-wide basis. This analysis will produce a strategic plan that will guide the Department in reconfiguring the Program to deal with the growing pool of restoration funds, to streamline operations, and to maximize restoration outcomes. The analysis will seek to identify staffing constraints and process bottlenecks in the course of achieving restoration, most often in coordination with our co-trustee partners.

2015 Activity Performance:

In 2015, the Program will continue to focus its activities in support of trust resource restoration, and will through additional restoration support staff and resources, see increased restoration outputs and outcomes. Fiscal year 2015 planned performance targets include the restoration of 100,000 acres and 250 stream or shoreline miles, increases of 77,500 acres (+344%) and 70 stream or shoreline miles (+39%), respectively, over the 2014 plan goals. The Department and its co-trustees will accomplish these goals through the use of funds or in-kind services received in settlement of damage assessment claims with responsible parties.

Upon completion of the detailed programmatic analysis and development of a strategic plan in late summer of 2014, the Department will implement the strategic plan to markedly increase the amount of acres and stream/shoreline miles being restored across the country, and to effectively utilize the growing balance of restoration settlement funds in the DOI Restoration Fund.

In addition to these activities, the RSU staff will lead technology transfer and outreach activities to ensure that restoration advances made by individual case teams will be shared with fellow restoration practitioners. Examples include participation on the team developing a Restoration Training class that will be taught at the FWS National Conservation Training Center. This pilot class is scheduled for August 2014 and will include modules specifically targeted at NRDAR restoration specialists. In addition, the RSU is organizing sessions for the Restoration Program's biennial workshop that include topics on Climate Change Impacts to Restoration Projects and Tribal Restoration Successes. The RSU will also continue to maintain its partnerships with the Society for Ecological Restoration (SER) and the Society of Environmental Toxicology and Chemistry (SETAC), and they will continue to develop and implement policies and guidance to coordinate NRD restoration planning and NEPA compliance actions.

The RSU will continue to work with the U.S. Geological Survey (USGS) to implement restoration science advances. Scientists from the USGS are working with the Restoration Support Unit in developing protocols to improve the monitoring and management of restoration projects and the development of effective measures of restoration success on historically contaminated lands. Because ecosystems are dynamic, restoration monitoring protocols must serve as triggers for corrective actions and adaptive management and be carefully crafted into restoration plans. USGS and the RSU are working with restoration scientists in the public and private sector to develop a primer for restoration monitoring that will provide the guidance necessary to ensure successful restorations and return ecosystem services to injured resources. These efforts are focusing on species distributions, abundance and diversity, invasive species, community development and, when possible, ecosystem resiliency which is critically important as the NRDAR program addresses the influence of global climate change on restoration planning, the role of global climate change in environmental responses to chemical exposure, how climate change may affect the damage assessment process, and to explore how restoration activities may aid in the adaptation and mitigation of climate change effects in our environment.

The RSU and USGS are also working with SER to highlight Departmental restoration projects on the SER Global Restoration Network website (http://www.globalrestorationnetwork.org/), a freely accessible internet-based platform where practitioners as well as stakeholders and the general public can go to obtain extensive information on restoration successes and lessons learned in the process. By documenting restoration activities and their ultimate success, the Program can maintain transparency in the process that returns ecosystem services lost as a result of chemical contamination.

These efforts bring USGS science expertise to address the ecological restoration of species and habitats injured by the release of oil or other hazardous substances and the monitoring and measurement of restoration success. Although many scientifically valid techniques are available to document the extent and severity of injury to natural resources, restoration science is still in its infancy. Several interconnected efforts, engaging multiple disciplines within USGS, are being undertaken to strengthen the state of restoration science, reduce disagreements with responsible parties, and help us achieve more timely and effective restoration.

RESTORING INJURED RESOURCES

Following an oil spill or the release of a hazardous material, the Natural Resource Trustees evaluate the injury to our trust resources and then write a restoration plan to outlines the projects that will be conducted to restore the injured resource. As part of the planning process, the public is invited to participate and provide comments on the restoration projects. The goal of the restoration projects is to restore the injured resource or the service lost as a result of the spill or release. For example, if an oil spill results in the destruction of beach dune habitat that is used by a shorebird for nesting, then restoration projects are designed to restore dune or beach habitat. Similarly, if the removal of a hazardous chemical from a wetland results in the loss of this wetland, then projects are designed to restore this wetland at its current location to its baseline condition or to replace or acquire similar habitat elsewhere.

The following are examples of recent on-the-ground restoration accomplishments achieved by the Department of the Interior's bureaus and their co-trustees. These examples are representative of the wide range of restoration actions that trustees may take to restore injured resources.

Nyanza Chemical Waste Dump, Massachusetts

The Nyanza Chemical Waste Dump is a 35-acre parcel of land located adjacent to an active industrial complex in Ashland, Massachusetts. Historical industrial operations at the site from 1917 to 1978 released large volumes of wastewater contaminated with organic and inorganic chemicals and acids. During the production of textile dyes, releases of mercury and chromium were of particular concern. Over 45,000 tons of chemical sludges, together with other chemical wastes, were buried on the site. Some of these wastes were discharged to the Sudbury River. As a result, groundwater, soils, sediments, and surface waters were contaminated with heavy metals and chlorinated organic compounds. The U.S. Environmental Protection Agency placed the Nyanza Chemical Waste Dump on the National Priorities List (Superfund) in 1983.

In 1998, the Nyanza Natural Resource Damages Trustee Council, comprised of the Massachusetts Executive Office of Energy and Environmental Affairs, U.S. Department of the Interior (through the Fish and Wildlife Service), and the National Oceanic and Atmospheric Administration reached a $ 3.7 million settlement for natural resources injured by hazardous substance released from the Nyanza Chemical Superfund site. These injuries include impacts to the Sudbury River, its flood plain. and the species that use this habitat, including songbirds and other birds, fish, amphibians, reptiles and mammals. The trustees have worked with numerous citizen, community, and environmental groups, as well as state and federal agencies to identify suitable restoration projects.

Restoration of native wild rice (*Zizania aquatica*), shown here along the Sudbury River in eastern Massachusetts, will be undertaken after controlling invasive aquatic vegetation. Native wild rice provides an important food source for migratory waterfowl and other birds in the Sudbury River watershed. (Photo credit: Ron McAdow, Sudbury Valley Trustees)

Eleven restoration projects benefitting the wildlife, landscape, and recreation and public access of the Sudbury River Watershed were funded by the settlement. When completed, these projects will provide the following benefits and services:

- restore migratory and coldwater fish habitat;
- protect land to conserve wildlife habitat;
- create public recreational access to the river through canoe access and improved trails and pathways;
- create a nature preserve;
- promote future river conservation through education programs such as the Sudbury River Schools Program;
- provide songbird habitat restoration, and
- control invasive aquatic weeds to improve recreation and wildlife habitats and diversity.

Additionally, to help restore wintering habitat for migratory songbirds impacted by the release, the Nyanza Trustees have directed a portion of settlement funds to the Belize Foundation for Research and Environmental Education (BFREE) to re-forest local Belize farms from intensive agricultural use to sustainable agro-forestry of shade-grown cacao. To date, three farmers have signed reforestation contracts and have begun planting cacao and other native trees. Other

32

contracts are being negotiated. This work will provide valuable wintering habitat for neo-tropical migratory songbirds in Central America.

Geo-locator device will allow the tracking and monitoring of songbird species to determine migration patterns in both Belize and New England. (Photo credit – Jackie Ricciardi)

Several of these projects, such as the control of aquatic weeds and the work being implemented by BFREE were begun in 2013. Additional projects should begin in 2014 and are expected to be completed over the next several years.

Tri-State Mining District / Cherokee County, Kansas

The Tri-State Mining District, which encompasses southeastern Kansas, southwestern Missouri, and northeastern Oklahoma, was extensively mined for over a century for zinc and lead, ranking first in terms of past zinc production in the United States and fourth in terms of past lead production. Past mining, milling, and processing activities resulted in the release of high levels of cadmium, lead, and zinc into the environment, and the degradation caused by mining resulted in the U. S. Environmental Protection Agency listing all three states mining-impacted areas on the National Priority List (Superfund) in 1983.

Cherokee County's landscape, once dominated by prairie, has been drastically transformed with development and farming. The continent's tallgrass prairie once covered approximately 400,000 square miles of North America; today it is estimated that less than one percent of the original tallgrass prairie remains. These remaining areas of native prairie are highly valued because they are among the most endangered ecosystems in the world. In addition, 69 species present in Cherokee County are included on state or Federal threatened and endangered species lists or are of special concern. The Spring River is one of the state's most valued surface water resources and supports at least 74 fish and 23 mussel species including the federally threatened Neosho madtom, the federally threatened rabbitsfoot mussel, and the federally endangered Neosho mucket mussel.

Native tallgrass prairie habitat acquired and protected by the Cherokee County trustees will benefit a variety of bird and mammal species. (Photo credit – John Miesner, FWS)

The U.S. Department of the Interior, represented by the Fish and Wildlife Service, and State of Kansas are the Trustees for the natural resources in Cherokee County. To date, the trustees have recovered over $14 million from responsible parties at the site. The vast majority of these funds (over $11 million) were recovered in a bankruptcy settlement with ASARCO, the largest responsible party at the site. To date, the Cherokee County trustees have used these funds to protect and/or restore a total of 3,625 acres. Additional parcels are also under consideration by the trustees and preliminary negotiations are underway. These projects are all targeted at restoring tall-grass prairie, wetlands, and riparian habitat which were damaged as the result of years of mining activities, ore processing, and disposal of waste tailings.

For example, 1,120 contiguous acres of real property in Cherokee and Labette counties were purchased by the trustees, which include wetland cells, restored native grass prairies, and existing riparian corridors to compensate for the injuries resulting from mining activities. Title to these properties is held by the state. Also, the trustees provided funds to purchase a tractor and related implements to be used by the state for the purpose of removing trees and other invasive vegetation which has resulted in the improvement of 2,350 acres of migratory bird habitat. The trustees have provided funds to convert 155 acres of fescue to native warm season grasses for the benefit of migratory birds on state property. The 155 acres that were restored was part of a larger restoration project implemented by the state that totaled 320 acres in size.

M/V Cosco Busan Oil Spill, California

The M/V Cosco Busan Oil Spill in San Francisco Bay, California on November 7, 2007 occurred when the container ship struck one of the towers of the San Francisco-Oakland Bay Bridge. This resulted in a large gash in the hull of the vessel, spilling 53,000 gallons of bunker fuel oil into the water killing nearly 7,000 birds and oiling their nesting and feeding habitats over 100 miles of shoreline, including beach and dune coastal habitat, and sensitive eel grass beds. In addition, the Golden Gate National Recreation Area, Point Reyes National Seashore, and the San Francisco Maritime National Historic Park were impacted by the oil.

In January 2012, a U.S. District Court approved the largest settlement in the history of the Oil Pollution Act. The $44.4 million settlement resolved all natural resource damages, penalties, and response costs that resulted from the spill. Of the total settlement, $23.6 million was deposited into the DOI Restoration Fund for the joint use of Federal and State trustees to restore injured natural resources in the spill area, including bird and habitat restoration, fish and eelgrass restoration, and recreational use improvements, consistent with a publicly reviewed restoration plan. An additional $7.3 million was awarded to the State trustees for recreational use improvements.

In 2013, $11 million in restoration funds were allocated to over 45 projects to restore the species and habitats injured by the spill, as well as to compensate the public for lost recreational uses. For example, several projects were aimed at reshaping, enhancing, and restoring beaches and habitat around the Bay Area. Muir Beach Dunes Restoration and the Visitor Access Improvements Projects at Golden Gate National Recreation Area received $2 million to restore recreational use and $215,000 for habitat restoration from the NRDA Trustee Council. This area has nearly 260,000 annual visitors. This project rerouted an existing beach access trail to decrease damage to the dunes, increase the dune restoration footprint, and improve accessibility. Invasive weeds on the dunes were reduced and re-vegetated with native dune plants. Visitors will see a new parking lot, an elongated 440-foot footbridge that sits over the wetlands and an interpretive exhibit on the local watershed. The old parking lots removal increases the flood plain from 50 to 450 feet and reintroduces a more natural water flow to the area.

A new parking lot and footbridge will improve visitor access at Muir Beach Dunes while increasing protection of sensitive dunes habitat. (Photo credit: Shirwin Smith, NPS)

The South Bay Salt Ponds Restoration project will provide high quality winter foraging habitat for small ducks and grebes at ponds within the Eden Landing Ecological Reserve. Levee road maintenance and installation of water control structures will allow pumping and annual management of water levels and water quality to benefit snowy plover nesting in the summer and small ducks and grebes during the fall and winter. Salinity levels will be monitored and adjusted through pond operations and management to provide the maximum benefit for these species.

Additionally, under the Marbled Murrelet Restoration project, the second year pilot study was completed in FY13 to address predation risk of murrelet eggs. Conditioned Taste Aversion (CTA) was the method used to train stellar jays to avoid marbled murrelet eggs. Jays that ingest the treated mimic eggs are expected to associate the unpleasant experience with murrelet eggs such that they modify their behavior and avoid ingesting actual murrelet eggs they encounter in the future. CTA was implemented in a phased approach, with initial experimental applications in Butano and Portola State Parks in the Santa Cruz Mountains. Marbled murrelets are federally listed as threatened under the Endangered Species Act.

ACTIVITY: INLAND OIL SPILL PREPAREDNESS

Oil spill response activities following the March 2013 Pegasus Pipeline Spill in Mayflower, Arkansas. A break in the pipeline released an estimated 5,000 – 7,000 barrels of heavy crude oil into the environment. (Photo Credit: Barry Forsythe, U.S. Fish and Wildlife Service)

Appropriation: Natural Resource Damage Assessment	2014 Enacted	Fixed Costs	Internal Transfers (+/-)	Program Changes (+/-)	2015 Request
Activity: Inland Oil Spill Preparedness	0	0	0	+1,000	1,000
FTE	0	0	0	+1	1

Justification of 2015 Program Changes:

Inland Oil Spill Preparedness ($1,000,000/+1 FTE) - The 2015 budget request for Inland Oil Spill Preparedness is $1,000,000 and 1 FTE, a program increase of $1,000,000 and 1 FTE from the 2014 enacted level. In the past few years, the Nation's domestic oil production has increased dramatically, largely due to the use of hydraulic fracturing technology to access deposits that were previously uneconomically recoverable. According to many experts, we are experiencing a domestic oil and gas renaissance that has transformed the Nation's energy future. In the next five to ten years, the U.S. will likely continue to greatly reduce its reliance on foreign oil and could become a net exporter of oil and gas. U.S. Energy Information Administration data show that, annual domestic oil production grew from approximately 1.8 billion barrels in 2008 to 2.3 billion barrels in 2012, an increase of 28 percent. During that year, DOI employees responded to over 900 oil spill incidents. Continued near-term growth is projected to reach 2.6 billion barrels in 2014.

Areas where oil and gas production have dramatically increased include:

- Increases in production of 135 percent in Midwestern states, and 48 percent in Rocky Mountain states;
- A production boom in the Bakken shale formation in North Dakota and Montana, where North Dakota oil production increased by 641 percent from 2000 to 2012;
- An increase of 65 percent in the Permian Basin (Texas & New Mexico) and the Western Gulf Basin (Texas) from 2000 to 2012.

This significant growth in domestic oil production has spurred a boom in pipeline construction to transport domestic oil from midwest and western oil fields and Canadian tar sands oil (bitumen) to Gulf Coast refineries. Since 2010, seven major pipeline projects have been completed in the U.S. consisting of new construction and other projects to expand capacity in existing pipelines. Further, a total of 13 new pipeline projects are expected to come online by the end of 2014 to deliver growing shipments of crude to Gulf Coast refineries and storage facilities.

Accelerating oil production in some areas is happening so fast that industry has turned to rail transport instead of waiting for pipelines to be constructed and transportation of oil by rail and truck has greatly increased. Data from the Association of American Railroads reveals the annual amount of oil transported by rail increased nearly 25-fold from 2008 to 2012, growing from 9,500 tanker cars to 233,800 tanker cars.

With the growth in oil production and transport comes the increased risk of spills that could impact public lands and resources under the trusteeship of the Department. Recent pipeline spills such as the ExxonMobil Yellowstone River spill in Montana (July 2011) and the ExxonMobil Pegasus Pipeline oil spill in Arkansas (March 2013) illustrate the real hazards of aging pipeline infrastructure, which accounted for 65 percent of the reported pipeline failures from 2002 to 2009. Likewise, rail transport oil spills increased by a factor of 11 from the 2007 – 2009 time period to the 2010 – 2012 time period. The Department, other government agencies, and various industries are working to improve efficiencies and environmental safeguards to address the related risks and challenges that come with increased domestic production and transportation. To ensure that the Department of the Interior and its bureaus are prepared to respond to potential spills, the Department must improve its inland oil spill preparedness and response capabilities.

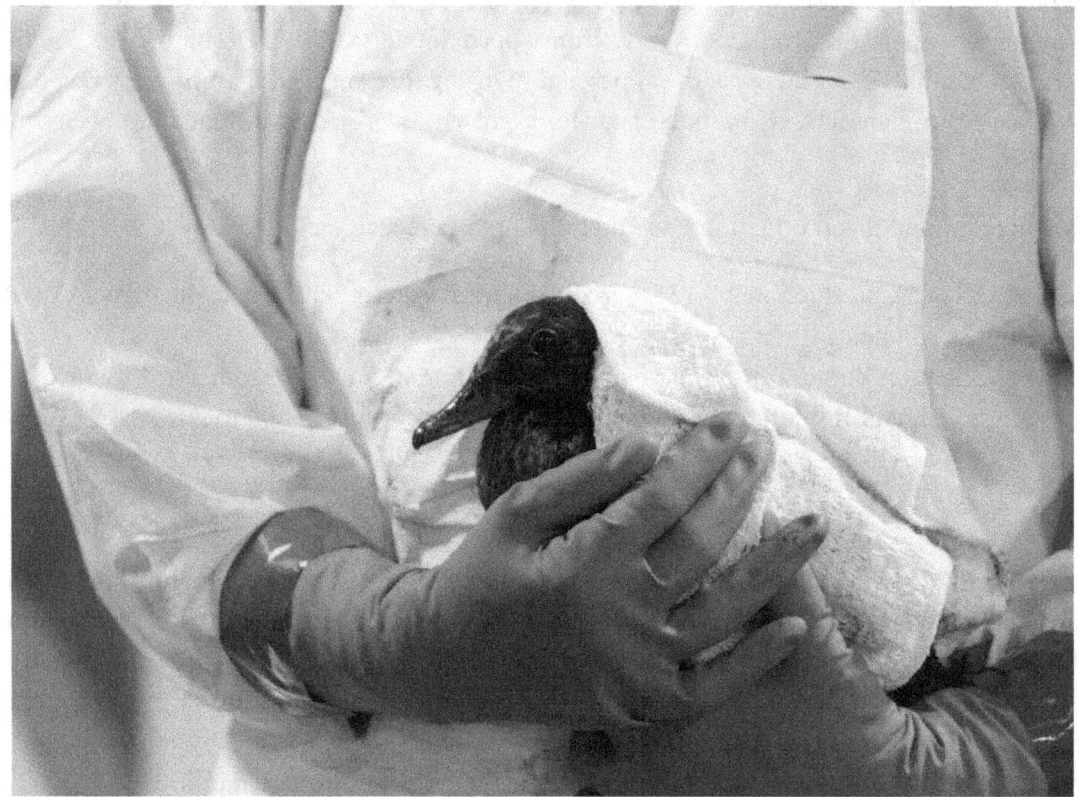

Cleaning an oiled duck collected following the March 2013 Pegasus Pipeline Spill in Mayflower, Arkansas. A break in the pipeline released an estimated 5,000 – 7,000 barrels of heavy crude oil into the environment. (Photo Credit: Mike Wintroath, Arkansas Game and Fish Commission).

Activity Overview:

In the current National Response System, EPA leads the federal response for inland oil spills and the U.S. Coast Guard leads the federal response for spills occurring offshore and in navigable waterways, including major rivers, lakes and bays. DOI is a primary Federal natural resource trustee with vast resources that could potentially be impacted by oil spills, including those managed by the National Parks Service, Fish and Wildlife Service, Bureaus of Land Management and Reclamation, and the trust lands and resources of Native American tribes. It is critical that DOI serve as a strong partner in the oil spill contingency planning process to address potential impacts to resources under the trusteeship and management of Interior Bureaus.

Discharges of oil and other hazardous substances from petroleum product production and transportation and inland facilities, including pipelines, can injure trust resources in a variety of ways. The Secretary of the Interior has trust responsibility for resources such as threatened and endangered species, national wildlife refuges, national parks, monuments, seashores, and historic sites, national conservation lands, reservoirs, reserved water rights, and certain Indian lands. When a spill occurs, employees of the Department's many Bureaus are often the first responders, along with State employees and EPA on scene coordinators. Pre-incident planning requires DOI employees to participate in local, regional and national contingency planning including contingency response teams, area contingency plans, and spill drills. It is this participation that will result in effective teamwork if a spill incident occurs. In addition, the Department's Incident Qualification and Certifications System (IQCS) and Resource Ordering and Status System (ROSS) provide critical support to oil spill incident responses.

The Department's Office of Environmental Policy and Compliance (OEPC) leads and coordinates DOI's participation on the National Response Team for both preparedness and response. One of its key activities is to coordinate DOI input to the Area Committee planning process, but DOI bureaus' budget constraints have limited their participation. While OEPC can provide generalized information regarding DOI resources, field-level expertise from the Bureaus is needed to identify specific areas for oil collection and deflection, as well avoidance areas for personnel and equipment. Lack of DOI bureau participation in EPA and U.S. Coast Guard led Area Committee meetings and exercises in prior years has resulted in (1) information gaps on DOI trust resources in Area Contingency Plans, (2) notification and communication challenges between EPA/U.S. Coast Guard and DOI during oil spill responses, and (3) unfamiliarity by DOI resource managers with oil spill response operations and organizations.

The program's objective is to improve DOI's overall preparedness and ability to respond to inland oil spills in ways that can better protect the Nation's natural and cultural resources, historic properties, and DOI lands, resources, and interests. The program will be a coordinated, integrated, cross-cutting effort involving FWS, NPS, USGS, BLM, BIA, BOR, and OEPC that will identify and support targeted work on Regional, Area, and Geographic Contingency Plans based on where the greatest risks and vulnerabilities exist that may adversely affect DOI lands, resources, and interests. Strong DOI engagement in the planning process is critical because these plans establish the response strategies that will be put into effect immediately by initial responders during the first few hours of an oil spill.

In addition, the program will support DOI Bureau field staff's participation in Area Committee oil spill response exercises alongside EPA and USCG staff, to experience and learn oil spill response organizations and operations, the roles of the on scene coordinator and the RRT, and build necessary relationships to work effectively towards protecting DOI trust resources when an oil spill occurs.

In 2015, the Department is requesting funds to improve its inland oil spill response capability. The funds would be used to train employees in spill preparedness, including understanding response techniques, participation in contingency planning, and establishing and maintaining an operational program that will result in more timely and more effective Departmental response to inland oil spills.

2015 Activity Performance:

The program's performance will be evaluated and documented to ensure robust programmatic performance and to support evidence-based decision making. This increase will support a valuable multi-year DOI crosscutting program with OEPC's Environmental Safeguards Group (ESG) who will support the inland spill program, provide advice, and document its program activities.

The ESG and the Restoration Program are uniquely equipped to work with DOI bureaus and offices to implement this program to deliver products and activities that improve DOI's inland oil spill preparedness. It is important to avoid having each bureau and office pursue its own program independently with no coordination or leveraged efforts. By working together, DOI bureaus and offices can leverage efforts to optimize this program's performance.

The program would identify and support participation by field and regional contacts to bolster information in these plans regarding natural and cultural resources, historic properties, and DOI lands, resources, and interests which could be threatened by an inland oil spill. This information would be developed and updated using the Geospatial Platform to consolidate data from all of the DOI bureaus and offices and other federal agencies such as EPA and DOT's Pipeline Hazards Safety Materials Administration (PHMSA).

The DOI program will:

1. Provide resources to enable DOI bureau/office participation in Regional, Area, and Geographic committee planning activities;
2. Provide resources to enable DOI bureau/office participation in inland oil spill response exercises and drills held by the EPA, U.S. Coast Guard, and National or Regional Response Teams;
3. Develop an online library of applicable guidance, templates, and technical resources related to contingency planning and response activities; and
4. Provide resources and develop targeted training to support effective engagement in inland oil spill contingency planning and response activities, with a special emphasis on highlighting protective measures for our natural and cultural resources and tribal lands.

ACTIVITY: PROGRAM MANAGEMENT

Appropriation: Natural Resource Damage Assessment		2014 Enacted	Fixed Costs	Internal Transfers (+/-)	Program Changes (+/-)	2015 Request
Activity: Program Management	$000	1,935	+18	0	+239	2,192
	FTE	7	0	0	0	7

Justification of 2015 Program Changes:

Program Management (+239,000) - The 2015 budget request for Program Management is $2,192,000 and 7 direct FTE, a program increase of $239,000 from the 2014 enacted level. The increase will be used to provide additional funding for bureau support positions in the five trustee bureaus (known as the Restoration Program Workgroup) and those bureaus and offices that provide technical support to the Departmental program. The Program currently provides $85,000 (approximately 0.6 allocation FTE) to each participating bureau and office for Workgroup participation and program support to match the recent growth in the number and size of settlements and restoration workload.

Activity Overview:

Program Management provides the strategic vision, direction, management, and coordination of inter-Departmental activities necessary for the Department to carry out the Restoration Program. It manages the intersection and complex interdisciplinary relationships between biology, environmental toxicology, natural resource management, economics, and law. The Program Management activity allocates damage assessment project funding; monitors program performance and ensures accountability; provides the framework for identifying and resolving issues that raise significant management or policy implications; develops the Department's policies and regulations for conducting and managing damage assessment and restoration cases; responds to Departmental, Office of Management and Budget, and Congressional inquiries; and ensures coordination among Federal, State, and Tribal governments.

Program Management funding enables the program to maintain support for bureau Workgroup representation, ensuring essential integrated program coordination across the Department. The request includes funds for program support positions in the five bureaus with primary trust resource management roles (BIA, BLM, BR, FWS, and NPS) and technical support offices (USGS, Office of Policy Analysis, and the Office of the Solicitor). A fully integrated Departmental program requires a significant level of bureau participation on the Workgroup and

Program Management Team, as well as continued regional coordination and technical support in science, economics, and law.

The Restoration Program Office will continue its ongoing efforts to enhance its outreach to Tribes in two significant ways. First, it continues its monthly conference calls with any tribal co-trustees that have an interest in the natural resources and restoration activities of the Department. Secondly, the program has begun a Tribal training initiative where it is partnering with the interested tribal co-trustees to design natural resource damage assessment (NRDA) training for tribal members and technical consultants. This effort will attempt to utilize existing Departmental and tribal training resources, educators, and experts to develop a curriculum and materials that are targeted to tribal resources in a NRDA context. Coincident to the Program improving relationships with Tribal co-trustees and governments, is an equally effort to maintain and improve communications with State co-trustees through the continued implementation of a Memorandum of Understanding (MOU) with the Association of Fish & Wildlife Agencies (AFWA). The AFWA MOU will facilitate communications between the Program and the State co-trustee on issues of mutual interest, with the intent of leading to the development of policies, improved assessment techniques, sharing of best practices, and if needed, regulatory revisions.

The Department continues to participate in collaboration and dialogue with the International Group of Protection and Indemnity Clubs (P&I Clubs), consistent with the 2012 Memorandum of Understanding (MOU) to agree to consider appropriate cooperative damage assessment activities during marine spill incidents involving vessels for which they insure (about 95% of all vessels afloat).

The Restoration Program Office continues to expand the deployment and use of information technology tools in 2014, including increased use of video-conferencing and developing program document libraries and document collaboration tools on the Program's SharePoint site. These improvements and the enhanced use of information technology by the Program Office has resulted in reduced travel costs, consistent with Secretarial and Administration priorities, while increasing internal communications efficiency.

2015 Program Performance:

All current Program Management efforts and activities are focused on providing the tools, processes, or infrastructure to achieve restoration of injured natural resources. In 2015, in compliance with Administration's Executive Order on *Campaign to Cut Waste*, the Program Office will seek to meet target goals by broadening its use of information technology in communicating with the program's Workgroup, Bureaus, State, Tribal, and other Federal agency partners as follows:

- Combining the use of DOI video conferencing, webinar, and SharePoint enterprise software technology. This technology will be used for all monthly meetings of the Program's Workgroup to discuss program and policy issues affecting new and ongoing damage assessment projects and policies. It will also be used for the annual allocation of funding for assessment projects, eliminating face-to-face meetings in DC and/or Denver and, thereby saving travel expenses and time of Workgroup members.

- The SharePoint enterprise software has been developed into a case Record Management System for the Program Office, affording Departmental bureaus and offices access to historical documents, including funding proposals dating back to 1999 as well as the attendant allocation memoranda and other supporting program documents. The Program's document library within the SharePoint system currently contains over 2,500 documents that have been generated by this program such as Pre-Assessment Screen, Assessment Plans, Restoration Plans, and Consent Decrees. All of these documents are stored in the library in "searchable" .pdf file format. What was previously a vast collection of information is becoming useful data that is organized and searchable.

- The organization and standardization of damage assessment project data allows the Program to track assessment project performance and the attainment of important case milestones. Such project performance data serves as an objective basis for future funding decisions.

- Enhanced and improved presentation and information on the Program's website (http://www.doi.gov/restoration) by improved design, accessibility, and content. A calendar of events feature has been added to inform the public of upcoming events related to public review of assessment and restoration plans, public meetings, and restoration site openings.

The 2015 request level will support the broadened Departmental communication, consultation, and coordination activities with Federal, State, and Tribal co-trustees, the environmental community, industry and the public. Continued cooperation and coordination with co-trustees is critical to increasing restoration productivity, and will enhance opportunities for efficiencies and to identify and eliminate duplication of effort and process redundancies.

Program management activities in 2015 will also continue efforts to develop, refine, and update a number of existing administrative and policy tools, with an eye towards improved consistency, effectiveness, and maximizing restoration outcomes. Among these efforts are the following:

- Continue to evaluate the appropriate role and use of economic analytical tools used in damage assessment and restoration activities.

- Coordinate with other trustees and restoration funding entities (namely the U.S. Coast Guard's National Pollution Funds Center) to continue the development of common cost documentation practices and formats to ensure consistency and uniformity.

- Broaden the opportunities for cooperative assessment by improving existing guidance and documents.

- Continue improvement of public outreach and information sharing through internet-based applications and websites.

- Adopt procedures that promote coordination between response and NRDAR activities.

- Ensure that compliance by federal trustees with the requirements of the National Environmental Policy Act (NEPA) occurs concurrently with restoration planning.

- Enhance its NRDAR partnerships with academia and non-governmental organizations, through improvements in grants, cooperative agreements, and contracting.

- Encourage the use of existing local and regional restoration plans and databases for use in NRDAR restoration efforts.

Continued development and broader use of these and other tools will help ensure cross-bureau consistency and compatibility of information and systems, allowing the program to serve as a model for integrated Department-wide natural resources management.

The Program continues to enjoy a good relationship with the other Federal agencies involved in NRDAR activities either directly (i.e. NOAA, Forest Service, and NPFC) or indirectly (i.e. EPA and DOE). The Program will explore opportunities for additional collaboration and coordination, particularly in the area of project prioritization and selection. In 2015, the program will continue to reach out to industry by participating in industry symposia and discussion groups on NRDAR issues and policy, and encouraging the use of cooperative damage assessments.

As a cost-saving measure in response to diminished travel budgets, the Restoration Program has transitioned from sponsoring its annual national workshop to a biennial schedule. The 2014 workshop has been approved. In recent years, this workshop has provided training for over 180 practitioners from across the Department on a variety of topics including project management, damage claim development, restoration methods and other scientific and legal issues. As an indicator of collaborative approach that continues to be pursued by the Department and its co-trustees, over 50 State, Tribal, and Federal co-trustees, as well as representatives from industry and the conservation community also attended the most recent workshop.

Program Support of Bureau, Department, and Government-wide Costs:

Section 404 of the 2014 Consolidated Appropriations Act directs the disclosure of overhead, administrative, and other types of administrative support spending. The provision requires that budgets disclose current amounts and practices with regard to overhead charges, deductions, reserves, or holdbacks from program funding to support government-wide, Departmental, or bureau administrative functions or headquarters, regional, or central office operations. Changes to such estimates trigger reprogramming procedures, in which the Department must provide advance notice to and seek approval from the House and Senate Appropriations Committees.

For 2015, the Restoration Program's costs related to overhead, administration, and central/regional operations are addressed in three components of the budget, all under the heading of External Administrative Costs. These costs include amounts paid to bureaus, the Department, or other Executive Branch agencies to support bureau, Departmental or Government-wide administrative costs.

External Administrative Costs
(Dollars in Thousands)

	FY 2013 Actual	FY 2014 Enacted	FY 2015 Request
DOI Working Capital Fund			
Centralized Billings	99	121	96
Fee for Services	0	0	0
Direct Billings (Financial Mgmt)	165	139	135
Reimbursables	0	0	0
Total, DOI Working Capital Fund	264	260	231
DOI Interior Business Center			
Financial Managment Systems Support	9	9	9
Fish and Wildlife Service			
FWS User-Pay Cost Share	827	140	140
Bureau of Safety and Environmental Enforcement			
Personnel / HR Services	20	25	25
U.S. Geological Survey			
Common Services Support	45	50	50
U.S. Department of Justice			
DOJ Sec. 108 3% Offset Authority	62	100	100

Charges related to the Departmental Working Capital Fund (WCF) identified in the preceding table reflect the Restoration Program's share of centralized Departmental expenses for items and expenses such as telecommunications, information technology management, security, mailroom services, costs associated with audited financial statements, and other WCF charges.

The Fish and Wildlife Service (FWS) levies its User-Pay Cost Share charges on damage assessment and restoration funds provided to the Service from the Restoration Program. Funds collected by FWS are used to offset a range of Service-wide administrative costs. For 2014, User-Pay Cost Share charges to the Restoration Program will be $140,421. The amounts identified for FY 2013 and 2014 are estimates based on prior year workload, and the actual amounts recovered may be more or less, depending upon actual workload, the timing of settlements, and the ability to recover such costs through settlement negotiations. Indirect costs will not be assessed to previous settlements or in cases where FWS indirect costs were not included or recovered in the final settlement. For 2015, FWS currently estimates those charges payable by the DOI Restoration Program to be comparable to the 2014 charges.

Charges related to the Bureau of Safety and Environmental Enforcement identified in the preceding table reflect the Restoration Program's share of personnel management and human resources (HR) services provided to the Office of the Secretary, covering items such as HR policies and procedures, staffing and delegated examining, employee classification, SES appointments, personnel security, reorganizations, and reductions-in-force.

The U.S. Geological Survey (USGS) applies a seven percent administrative overhead charge to all funds provided to USGS, primarily to the Columbia Environmental Research Center. Funds collected by the Center are used to offset common client administrative and facility expenses. Funds provided to USGS from the Exxon Valdez Oil Spill settlement include a nine percent general administrative assessment.

The Department of Justice applies a three percent offset to some, but not all, civil litigation debt collections made on behalf of the Restoration Program. Authority for these offsets can be found in Section 108 of the Commerce, Justice, and State Appropriations Act for Fiscal Year 1994 (P.L. 103-121, 107 Stat 1164 (1994). The offset is applicable to collections where the Department is the sole recipient of the funds. Funds subject to the offset authority are credited to the DOJ Working Capital Fund. The DOJ offset authority does not apply to restoration settlements jointly shared with non-Federal co-trustees that are collected by DOJ and deposited into the DOI Restoration Fund.

The Program Management activity, which includes Restoration Program administrative functions and central and regional operations, does not assess or levy any internal program overhead charges, deductions, or holdbacks to support such program operations.

DEPARTMENT OF THE INTERIOR
NATURAL RESOURCE DAMAGE ASSESSMENT AND RESTORATION
RESTORATION FUND

Program and Financing (in thousands of dollars)

Identification code 14-1618-0-1-302	2013 Actual	2014 Enacted	2015 Request
Obligations by program activity:			
Direct Program:			
0001 Damage Assessments	21,890	13,000	12,000
0002 Prince William Sound Restoration	3,045	2,000	2,000
0003 Other Restoration	48,796	60,000	62,000
0004 Program Management	4,497	3,000	3,000
0005 Oil Spill Preparedness	0	0	1,000
0900 Total, Direct program	78,228	78,000	80,000
Budgetary resources available for obligation:			
1000 Unobligated balance carried forward, Oct. 1	540,252	532,363	605,920
1010 Unobligated balance transferred to other accounts	-1,907	-6,000	-6,000
(Funds Transferred to DOC/NOAA 13-4316)	[-1,777]	[-6,000]	[-6,000]
(Funds Transferred to Forest Service 12-9921)	[-130]	[0]	[0]
1020 Unobligated balance transferred from other accounts			
(Funds Transferred from DOI/NPS 14-1039)	564	0	0
1021 Recoveries of prior year unpaid obligations	1,284	0	0
1050 Unobligated balance (total)	540,193	526,363	599,920
Budget Authority			
Appropriations, discretionary			
1100 Appropriation	6,253	6,263	7,767
Appropriations, mandatory			
1201 Appropriation (Special fund)	68,502	80,000	80,000
1220 Appropriation transferred to other accounts	-4,153	-6,000	-6,000
(Funds Transferred to DOC/NOAA 13-4316)	[-4,103]	[-6,000]	[-6,000]
(Funds Transferred to Forest Service 12-9921)	[-50]	[0]	[0]
1230 Appropriations permanently reduced	-204	-706	0
1260 Appropriations (mandatory) total	64,145	73,294	74,000
1900 Budget Authority (total)	70,398	79,557	81,767
1930 Total budgetary resources available	610,591	605,920	681,687
Memorandum (non-add) entries:			
1941 Unobligated balance carried forward, end of year:	532,363	605,920	681,687

DEPARTMENT OF THE INTERIOR
NATURAL RESOURCE DAMAGE ASSESSMENT AND RESTORATION
RESTORATION FUND

Program and Financing (in thousands of dollars)

Identification code 14-1618-0-1-302	2013 Actual	2014 Enacted	2015 Request
Change in obligated balance:			
Obligated balance, start of year (net):			
3000 Unpaid obligations, brought forward, Oct. 1 (gross)	25,951	21,798	21,798
3030 Obligations incurred, unexpired accounts	-4,153	[-6,000]	[-6,000]
3040 Outlays, gross (-)	0	0	0
3080 Recoveries of prior year unpaid obligations (-)	0	0	0
Obligated balance, end of year (net):			
3090 Unpaid obligations, end of year (gross)	21,798	21,798	21,798
3100 Obligated balance, end of year (net)	21,798	21,798	21,798
Budget authority and outlays, net:			
Discretionary:			
4000 Budget authority, gross	6,253	6,263	7,767
Outlays, gross			
4010 Outlays from new discretionary authority	2,575	4,384	5,437
4011 Outlays from discretionary balances	2,174	1,876	1,879
4020 Outlays, gross (total)	4,749	6,260	7,316
Mandatory:			
4090 Budget authority, gross	64,145	73,294	74,000
Outlays, gross			
4100 Outlays from new mandatory authority	5,720	6,000	7,000
4101 Outlays from mandatory balances	62,955	* 70,000	68,000
4110 Outlays, gross (total)	68,675	76,000	75,000
Net budget authority and outlays:			
4180 Budget authority	70,398	79,557	81,767
4190 Outlays	73,424	82,260	82,316
Investments in U.S. securities			
5000 Total investments, start of year			
U.S. securities, par value	134,135	484,753	490,000
5001 Total investments, end of year			
U.S. securities, par value	484,753	490,000	490,000

* NOTE: FY 2014 outlays from mandatory balances incorrectly shown as $7 million in MAX due to typographic error

DEPARTMENT OF THE INTERIOR
NATURAL RESOURCE DAMAGE ASSESSMENT AND RESTORATION
RESTORATION FUND

Program and Financing (in thousands of dollars)

Identification code 14-1618-0-1-302	2013 Actual	2014 Enacted	2015 Request
DIRECT OBLIGATIONS			
Personnel compensation:			
11.1　Full-time permanent	946	1,150	1,600
11.3　Other than full-time permanent	61	30	30
11.5　Other personnel compensation	22	10	10
11.9　　Total personnel compensation	1,029	1,190	1,640
12.1　Civilian personnel benefits	313	400	625
21.0　Travel and transportation of persons	30	30	35
22.0　Transportation of things	20	2	2
23.1　Rental payments to GSA	28	200	200
23.3　Communications, utilities, & misc. charges	8	7	7
24.0　Printing and reproduction	0	2	2
25.2　Other services	7	100	100
25.3　Purchases of goods & services from other govt. accts	24,137	14,700	15,000
26.0　Supplies and materials	6	15	10
31.0　Equipment	6	10	10
42.0　Insurance claims and indemnities	11,432	14,750	15,000
99.9　Subtotal, direct obligations	37,016	31,406	32,631
ALLOCATION ACCOUNTS			
Personnel compensation:			
11.1　Full-time permanent	8,116	8,000	8,000
11.3　Other than full-time permanent	2,364	2,600	2,600
11.5　Other personnel compensation	330	300	300
11.8　Special personnel services payment	9	0	0
11.9　Total personnel compensation	10,819	10,900	10,900
12.1　Civilian personnel benefits	3,242	3,400	3,469
21.0　Travel and transportation of persons	936	900	1,000
22.0　Transportation of things	86	10	10
23.1　Rental payments to GSA	93	100	100
23.2　Rental payments to others	169	150	150
23.3　Communications, utilities, & misc. charges	90	95	100
24.0　Printing and reproduction	21	15	15
25.1　Advisory and assistance services	8	24	25
25.2　Other services	13,865	15,600	15,800
25.3　Purchases of goods & services from other govt. accts	1,739	1,900	1,900
25.4　Operation & maintenance of facilities	0	50	50
25.5　Research and development contracts	1	50	50
25.7　Operation & maintenance of equipment	92	50	50
26.0　Supplies and materials	499	550	550
31.0　Equipment	1,098	200	200
32.0　Land and structures	2,726	2,900	3,000
41.0　Grants	5,727	9,700	10,000
42.0　Insurance claims and indemnities	1	0	0
99.0　Subtotal obligations - Allocation Accounts	41,212	46,594	47,369
99.9　Total new obligations	78,228	78,000	80,000

DEPARTMENT OF THE INTERIOR
NATURAL RESOURCE DAMAGE ASSESSMENT AND RESTORATION
RESTORATION FUND

Program and Financing (in thousands of dollars)

Identification code 14-1618-0-1-302	2013 Actual	2014 Enacted	2015 Request
Obligations are distributed as follows:			
Natural Resource Damage Assessment Program Office	37,016	31,406	32,631
Bureau of Indian Affairs	940	1,000	1,000
Bureau of Land Management	719	700	700
Bureau of Reclamation	42	55	55
Fish and Wildlife Service	24,901	33,439	34,214
National Park Service	7,513	7,000	7,000
Office of the Secretary	864	400	400
U.S. Geological Survey	6,233	4,000	4,000
99.9 Total new obligations	78,228	78,000	80,000

Personnel Summary

Identification code 14-1618-0-1-302	2013 Actual	2014 Enacted	2015 Request
Direct:			
Total compensable workyears:			
1001 Full-time equivalent employment	9	10	14

DEPARTMENT OF THE INTERIOR
NATURAL RESOURCE DAMAGE ASSESSMENT AND RESTORATION
EMPLOYEE COUNT BY GRADE

	2013 Actual	2014 Enacted	2015 Request
Executive Level	0	0	0
SES..	1	1	1
CA-3 *...	0	0	0
AL-2-3 **.......................................	0	0	0
SL-0 ***..	0	0	0
subtotal..............	1	1	1
GS/GM-15	0	1	1
GS/GM-14	2	2	2
GS/GM-13	4	3	4
GS-12	0	2	4
GS-11	1	1	2
GS-10	0	0	0
GS-9	1	0	0
GS-8	0	0	0
GS-7	0	0	0
GS-6	0	0	0
GS-5	0	0	0
GS-4	0	0	0
GS-3	0	0	0
GS-2	0	0	0
subtotal (GS/GM)..............	8	9	13
Total employment (actual / projected) at end of fiscal year......................	9	10	14

*CA - DOI Board Member
**AL - Administrative Law Judge
***SL - Senior-Level / Scientific Professionals

www.ingramcontent.com/pod-product-compliance
Lightning Source LLC
Chambersburg PA
CBHW080908290526
45795CB00007BA/2452